Royalty Publishing House is now accepting manuscripts from aspiring or experienced urban romance authors!

WHAT MAY PLACE YOU ABOVE THE REST:

Heroes who are the ultimate book bae: strong-willed, maybe a little rough around the edges but willing to risk it all for the woman he loves.

Heroines who are the ultimate match: the girl next door type, not perfect - has her faults but is still a decent person. One who is willing to risk it all for the man she loves.

The rest is up to you! Just be creative, think out of the box, keep it sexy and intriguing!

If you'd like to join the Royal family, send us the first 15K words (60 pages) of your completed manuscript to submissions@royaltypublishinghouse.com

Indian
Families
of the
Northwest
Coast

LIKE OUR PAGE!

Be sure to LIKE our Royalty Publishing House page on Facebook!

CPSIA information can be obtained
at www.ICGtesting.com
Printed in the USA
LVHW031734290719
625730LV00004B/882

Claudia Lewis

Indian Families of the Northwest Coast

The Impact of Change

The University of Chicago Press · Chicago and London

International Standard Book Number: 0-226-47686-5

Library of Congress Catalog Card Number: 70-108776

The University of Chicago Press, Chicago 60637
The University of Chicago Press, Ltd., London

© 1970 by The University of Chicago. All rights reserved

Published 1970

Printed in the United States of America

To the Indians
with Gratitude and Friendship

Contents

	PREFACE ix
1	THE SETTING, THE PROBLEM, AND THE APPROACH 3
2	BEFORE THE WHITE MAN 12
	LOCATION AND TERRAIN 13
	KINSHIP SYSTEM 15
	SOCIAL ORGANIZATION AND STATUS 18
	SPIRIT POWER 22
	SPIRIT DANCING 24
	OTHER USES OF THE SUPERNATURAL 27
	LIFE AFTER DEATH 30
	THE CYCLE OF LIFE 32
3	ENTER THE WHITE MAN 46
	THE FIRST FIFTY YEARS 46
	INTRODUCTION TO 1954 56
4	SETTLEMENT PATTERN AND SOCIAL ORGANIZATION, 1954 61
	OVERVIEW OF THE RESERVE 61
	SETTLEMENT PATTERN OF VILLAGE I 65
	BAND UNITY 72
	BEYOND THE RESERVE 77
	IN THE TOWN 80

CONTENTS

5   THREE HOUSEHOLDS   87
       THE OLD INDIAN WAYS: PAUL HARRY FAMILY   87
       BETWEEN THE OLD AND THE NEW:
          BILL GORDON HOUSEHOLD   96
       NEW WAYS: FRED WILSON FAMILY   104

6   FAMILY AND COMMUNITY LIFE   113
       THE CROWDED, CLUTTERED HOUSEHOLD   113
       THE WOMEN OF THE HOUSE:
          PERSISTENCE OF OLD ROLES   119
       MARRIAGES   125
       LIVES OF MEN: THE CYCLE OF POVERTY
          AND DEPENDENCE   141
       THE SEARCH FOR STATUS   146
       YOUNG PEOPLE: OLD WAY OR NEW?   163
       THE CHILDREN AND THEIR CHALLENGE   169

7   THE NEW WAY: IMPLICATIONS, RECOMMENDATIONS, PREDICTIONS   180

       EPILOGUE: SUMMER 1968   197

       INDEX   221

Preface

In 1950 and 1951, as a member of the Doukhobor Research Committee chaired by the anthropologist Harry B. Hawthorn of the University of British Columbia, I made a study of Doukhobor childhood and family life, now published as a chapter in *The Doukhobors of British Columbia*.[1] In 1954 Dr. Hawthorn, knowing of my interest in pursuing further studies of family and community life, suggested that I join forces for a summer with one of his graduate students, Elizabeth Lok, who had an assignment on a survey of social and economic conditions undertaken by the university's "Indian Research Project" staff for the Department of Citizenship and Immigration, Indian Affairs Branch.[2] I followed Dr. Hawthorn's suggestion, and in this way the present study had its inception. Elizabeth Lok and I settled down for the summer of 1954 with the "Camas" Indians on Vancouver Island, she to work on the survey and I to gather

1. H. B. Hawthorn, ed., "Childhood and Family Life" (Vancouver: The University of British Columbia, and J. M. Dent and Sons [Canada], 1955), pp. 97–121.
2. For the results of this survey see H. B. Hawthorn, C. S. Belshaw, and S. M. Jamieson, eds., *The Indians of British Columbia: A Study of Contemporary Social Adjustment* (Berkeley and Los Angeles: University of California Press, 1958).

my own data, the two of us collaborating informally in a way that we both found very helpful. I made a brief return alone in the summer of 1957.

In the body of this book I am presenting the material as I first conceptualized it, following these two summer visits. (Unless specific mention is made of 1957, however, all reporting refers to 1954.) The Epilogue, written after a return in the summer of 1968, offers the opportunity to amplify, check, and view change in the making.

Actually, a short return was made in 1965, also. Unexpectedly finding myself in the area, I arranged to stop over for a day. This was only long enough to talk briefly with officials in the Indian Office about new developments and to look up a few of my Indian friends. This short return was more a matter of friendship than of follow-up. In my own mind it merges with the return of 1968; and therefore, it will not be treated separately.

The true name of the Indian band is disguised in this book, as are names of individuals and all villages and towns in the immediate locale. Though it might be a contribution to anthropology to identify families, as has been done in the past in this area, I feel that the gain will outweigh the loss. The Indians here under consideration are no longer an isolated primitive group. A study of their life today is a study of the human dynamics of a group of citizens. I want to put the emphasis on "human," and accord due respect to these people among whom I have lived as friend. Furthermore, my major purpose is not so much to provide a case study of this specific community as it is to present a method, a way of approach, that may be applied in comparable situations. I believe that a community study has value to the extent that it demonstrates ways of exploring problems and discovering those interconnections that clarify meanings.

I am grateful to many people who gave me assistance and cooperation; particularly, of course, to Dr. Hawthorn. He not only introduced me to Elizabeth Lok and to the Indian community, but greatly stimulated and enriched my thinking on the occasions when I discussed my early findings with him.

PREFACE

I am also indebted to Solon T. Kimball, who was then at Teachers College, and Conrad M. Arensberg of the Anthropology Department of Columbia University, where I was pursuing doctoral study in the 1950s. Both gave me invaluable help in constructing the basic framework of my research.

My gratitude goes also to the officials in the local Indian Office who cooperated with me so fully and graciously and to the other town residents who gave me information. Because of my wish to disguise the locality, these individuals must go unnamed.

Especially I am indebted to the Indians themselves. During these fourteen years I have come to think of many of them as friends; I am personally concerned over their problems; and I hope to follow their fortunes for many years to come. This candid book about their lives is written in a spirit of respect and with the hope that its insights may serve a useful purpose wherever others are facing similar problems.

Indian
Families
of the
Northwest
Coast

1

The Setting, the Problem, and the Approach

The disorganization that often accompanies the impact of modern life on Indian groups in America is a well-known phenomenon, consisting of a complex of problems not uncommon wherever dark-skinned minority groups are gradually—or sometimes precipitously—taking on the culture of a White majority, or wherever such minorities feel themselves relegated to a separate and unequal way of life.

A particularly fruitful laboratory for the study of social dilemmas such as these exists on the east coast of Vancouver Island, where a large band of Salish Indians (872 members in 1954) lives on a reserve adjacent to one of the island's small prosperous municipalities, a few miles north of Victoria.

Even a casual visitor to the town, though he may have only a layman's concern for family life, can scarcely fail to wonder at some of the street scenes, and to ask himself whether all is as well as it might be with the Indians of this region.

At half-past nine on a rainy Saturday night in August he may see a young Indian woman with a baby in her arms and three small children beside her, huddling on the steps of the building next to one of the beer parlors. She is, of course, waiting for her man to come out, so they can drive to their home five miles or so across the reserve.

Or on the opposite side of the street, at the other beer parlor, the visitor sees a family encamped in a somewhat different fashion. In their parked car outside, the Indian father sits awhile with the fretting baby, while the mother goes inside and has her drinks. When she comes out to the car to do her stint of baby-sitting, the father goes in. When the child falls asleep, he is left alone in the car.

As the automobiles pull out at the beer parlor's closing time, the observer may wonder how many of the Indians who have been sitting there drinking for hours on this particular Saturday will make the trip home safely. They may be driving several miles, not only on this reserve but to the neighboring small reserves up and down the coast. The local newspaper not infrequently carries notices such as this of 18 July 1957 concerning an Indian driver:

> Mrs. C—— T——, of W——, pleaded guilty Wednesday to a charge that she drove on the Trans-Canada Highway while impaired by alcohol Tuesday evening.
>
> She had been apprehended after a minor accident with another car, and had failed to stop. . . .
>
> L—— S——, also of W——, and a passenger in Mrs. T——'s car, was charged with having a bottle of gin and a case of beer in her possession.
>
> Magistrate B—— fined her $10 and $4.40 costs.
>
> Her case was dealt with under the Indian Act.

If the observer is a visitor in the fall, he may wonder at the long line of Indian men queued up at the Indian Agency's office to ask for relief upon their return from the annual summer trek to the berry fields across the line in the state of Washington. "What did they do with the money they earned picking berries?" he wonders.

If the observer drives down to the bay on one of the woodland roads running through the reserve, the condition of some of the Indian houses he passes, and the values implicit concerning housekeeping and the roles of wife and mother, may puzzle him.

One house, for instance, of unfinished wood, looks sturdy

enough and rather new. It could be an attractive cabin on its beautiful forested plot of ground. Yet the porch and steps and surrounding yard area are so cluttered with objects—sacks, pans, tires, cloths, boots, toys, old motors, and cast-off pieces of furniture—that the eye can scarcely take it all in. Seven lively little children run in and out; their clothes are grimy with the dirt of play; their teeth are rotten; the youngest children are covered with scabby sores on their faces and heads and arms and legs.

The open door discloses a table crowded with crockery and objects of various kinds—cups, containers, jars, pop bottles, and a half-emptied quart of milk. It is as though a meal had just been finished and not cleared away. Against this backdrop, the mother of the family—a woman of about thirty-five—suddenly emerges. There on her crowded porch she stands, cigarette in hand. She wears a clean flowered print dress of silk or rayon, and she is sparkling in glassy costume jewelry. Her neat hair appears to have been cut and styled and permanent-waved in a beauty parlor.

Everywhere on the reserve the Indian children impress the observer with their liveliness, even their daring. They are not children who shrink away or timidly hide from the visitor. Instead, they may approach him, half friendly, half defiant. "So, you have come to look at the Indians?" Agile and seemingly fearless, children as young as eight, girls as well as boys, climb on the rails of a high bridge over the river; they spend long, happy summer days in the swimming hole, unsupervised except for the supervision older children exercise over younger. Independent at an early age, even a little six-year-old boy will seat himself all alone in one of the pews on the men's side, in the Catholic church on Sunday.

But these children, so attractive in their personalities, are on the other hand often neglected in appearance, with clothes unkempt, and teeth decayed. They are seen wandering around town eating chocolate bars and drinking pop.

Such observations as the foregoing are the superficial ones that any visitor might make, and of course they are one-sided and somewhat misleading. There are Indians on this reserve who never go near the beer parlor, whose neat homes are scarcely distinguishable from those of their White neighbors, whose breadwinners are fairly steady workers, whose children are kept immaculate and healthy.

In any group, at any given time, there are divergencies; and particularly among the Indians whose living members have experienced different phases of life on the reserve, there will be great differences across the generations, in the pace and ease of adaptation to modern ways. Other factors as well—always challenging to try to delineate—make for differences in circumstances and values, from family to family.

Nevertheless, such observations as the above are open to everyone to make and help to color the reputation of the Indian group here under study. What appears disreputable or decadent is usually easier to spot than behavior that seems more "normal."

That this particular Indian group has had a rather low reputation is indisputable, in spite of the fact that under the present very enlightened administration changes for the better seem to be under way. Officials in the local Indian Office have wondered why the men and women of this band—the largest of the fifteen in their agency—seek relief to the extent they do; why so many will give up a good job and go off to the berry fields in the summer; why many of them will not work at their longshoring and logging jobs even long enough to make themselves eligible for unemployment insurance; why so many get into fights when they come out of the beer parlors.

As for the opinions of the White residents of the area—"just siwash" is the way one professional man of seventy contemptuously characterized this Salish group, among whom he had lived and worked for the better part of his life. This is no doubt one of the extreme opinions, but even the casual visitor surveying the cluttered and desolate homes perched on their unkept acres, and aware of the White values centering on home and family, has some understanding of what is meant.

A sojourn of several weeks in the area, access to records in the office of the Indian Agency, and observations of a more than casual nature open more basic questions relative to the impact

SETTING, PROBLEM, AND APPROACH

of modern life on the Indians of this region. It soon becomes evident that the Indians are still carrying on "winter ceremonies" with a fairly full participation by the entire group. The researcher learns that the attractive young Indian girl—a public high school graduate—who is clerking in one of the town's largest stores was recently given an Indian "naming ceremony," along with her younger brother, in the traditional spectacular Indian style. According to her own report, this big winter ceremony must have cost her father about fifteen hundred dollars, considering the cost of the firewood for the bonfires on the earth floor of the Big House, the dinner to feed the hundreds of guests, the Hudson's Bay blankets and fifty-cent pieces given away ceremonially. Furthermore, a sixteen-year-old girl who is a graduate of the Catholic day school for Indians and has had a half year of high school in addition—a young girl dressed and groomed in the style of the young people of the town—recently was initiated as a "new dancer." The old rite, somewhat adapted to modern conditions, was carried out. The girl was kept in confinement in her home for the ritual period of four days and four nights, guarded by several women in turn, especially chosen for the purpose; her face was ritually painted. During the period of seclusion she found her "song," and then the appropriate costume, signifying her own song, was made for her. Night after night she danced and sang at the dances held in her honor, while her parents, aided by relatives and friends, took the responsibility to feed the guests and distribute gifts of sugar.

Not only are the Indians carrying on their own ceremonies —so totally at variance with the life of the White community at their doorstep—but in other aspects of their personal lives very divergent standards are operating. The researcher is soon not surprised to learn that one of the leading Indian citizens—a Catholic, as are most of the Indians here—has been living with his wife for years, and bringing up a large family of children, without sanction of legal marriage. Since a former wife "parted" from him, and was not dead, what else could he do? Furthermore, in even the younger generation, legal marriage before pregnancy, or before birth of a child or two, has been by no means the general rule.

The constitution of the family in the household, too, differs from the usual nuclear family pattern in the White man's town, the outstanding difference being the prominence of the grandmother as a rearer of children.

Thus the Indians live on the doorstep of the town, but are not really a part of it; their homes, it might be said, constitute an outlying slum of this well-kept little city of three thousand, center of a region famous for its beautiful residences, its prosperous farming, and logging industries. Jogging along in their own ways, clinging to their own old ceremonies, drinking up their earnings, or coming back broke after the binges in the berry fields, they pose serious problems for the administrators concerned with and responsible for their welfare, health, and education.

The present study is oriented toward these practical problems, but it will begin with the past rather than with the contemporary scene. Its fundamental premise is that the Indian pattern of life must be understood in terms of underlying motives and values; that there is indeed a pattern in the life of any group of people, making an intelligible whole of the kinship structure, economic life, social organization, religion, and arts—a whole which may be loosely knit and contain dysfunctional elements, yet has come into existence because it is useful and can serve as a vehicle for the satisfaction of needs and values.

Our first task is to illuminate the value-laden apparatus of the "Camas" Indians—as I call them—through examination of the interlocking institutions of the aboriginal culture. Then we will be in a position to think of the individual Indians of the present day—the man drinking away his earnings at the beer parlor, the woman in her cluttered home, the acculturated father who gives a "naming ceremony" for his children—as people who are coping with the problems of readjustment while modern life impinges upon them in this old domain of theirs, once their abundant, wild, wooded territory.

The study will concern itself with the over-all picture of Indian life, but at the hub will be the Indian community and family, the husband, wife, father, mother, and child, since it is within this network of personal relations that needs and values become crystallized; within this web that personality is shaped, the roles of the sexes and the generations find definition, and feelings about authority and status take root.

My effort in observing the contemporary scene has been to study "conditions in vivo," to use Arensberg's term, "in their full natural, living setting and relationships."[1] My informants consisted of all who would talk with me—by 1957 a total of some fifty Indians, not including children, and fifteen men and women of the White population, exclusive of the officials in the Indian Agency. Care was taken to include among the Indian informants both men and women, young, middle-aged, and old; to visit not only the more acculturated families who spoke English fluently, but also those less acculturated whose English was very halting; to speak not only with the chief and members of the council but with those holding less formal positions of leadership; to include Catholics, Protestants, and Shakers, drinkers and nondrinkers, dancers and nondancers, the steady workers and the itinerants, residents of the Indian village near the town and those living distant from the town; in short, a rough sample of the population.

Band lists provided information relative to kinship ties and other marriage and family data; and the role of the Indian Agency was thoroughly explored, with the full cooperation of the officials concerned.

"Event analysis"—that is, study of the settlement pattern and the comings and goings of individuals throughout the day, the interactions as they can be observed occurring in a pattern of both space and time—offered valuable clues to understanding, in my attempt to uncover unanticipated connections between phenomena.[2]

Good rapport with the Indians was established at the outset,

---

1. Conrad M. Arensberg, "The Community-Study Method," *American Journal of Sociology* 9 (September 1954): 111.
2. See Solon T. Kimball and Marion Pearsall, "Event Analysis as an Approach to Community Study," *Social Forces* 34 (October 1955): 58–63.

as I made my way around the reserve in the company of my companion from the University of British Columbia. Her purpose—to gather information to serve as a basis for recommendations for new administrative action—was made clear to the Indians, and was highly acceptable to the majority who were approached. Though my purposes differed in some respects, we often carried on joint interviews, and formed a team that was well received in both the Indian and the White community. It should be pointed out, however, that though we found the Indians friendly, we were unsuccessful in our efforts to rent a room in an Indian home for even a short period of a few days and nights. We were so regularly refused as we made our rounds searching for living quarters that we soon gave up the attempt and settled in an auto court at the edge of the reserve. We were told, kindly enough, that "my house isn't big enough," or "the lady up the hill has more room," or "my house is always filled with relatives," or "I'm having trouble with my teeth right now"—reasons which, in many cases, hardly seemed descriptive of the situation before our eyes. It is likely that embarrassments or suspicions lay behind the refusals, and it is possible, too, that some families may have feared overstepping permissible bounds, even though it was explained that we were seeking residence on the reserve with the chief's permission.

Our contacts with the Indians, then, did not include an intimate sharing of Indian home life. Information was gathered, instead, on the basis of afternoon or evening or morning calls, made sometimes by appointment, sometimes unannounced. Only one door was closed to us after we had knocked and stated our purposes. Though in some cases there was hesitance at the outset—"I don't speak English well"—and though sometimes we were not invited to enter the houses and had to converse on porches and front steps, in general the Indians who were approached were willing to answer questions and to enter into conversations. We were sometimes asked to make return visits; and when we encountered in the town Indians whom we knew, long street-corner chats were very easily initiated. At several homes we felt free to stop and talk at any time of the day, as we passed by on the way to town from the auto court, and the children of these homes were especially friendly with us, often accompanying us on our walks back and forth. There was no apparent resentment of our presence at any of the Indian group functions attended, such as church services and the funeral of a baby. Ready permission was granted to us by the chief in 1954 to carry on our interviewing program on the reserve; and when I returned to the auto court in 1957, the chief then also extended a gracious welcome.

As we turn now to look at the people and consider the problems of the Camas Reserve, an overview of the early culture as it functioned just before the entry of the White settlers will provide our introduction.

2

Before the White Man

The early culture of the Salish Indians of the Northwest Coast, including the Camas Band, has been fully studied and reported. In this chapter, I am relying chiefly upon Boas,[1] Curtis,[2] Barnett,[3] and Lane,[4] and also upon a paper, "[Camas] Indian Native Culture,"[5] prepared by an interested schoolteacher in the locality with the help of Indians themselves.

---

1. Franz Boas, "First General Report on the Indians of British Columbia," *Report of the Fifty-Ninth Meeting of the British Association for the Advancement of Science, 1889* (London: John Murray, 1891), pp. 801–55; and Franz Boas, "Second General Report on the Indians of British Columbia," *Report of the Sixtieth Meeting of the British Association for the Advancement of Science, 1890* (London: John Murray, 1891), pp. 563–82.
2. Edward S. Curtis, *Salishan Tribes of the Coast,* vol. 9 of 20 vols., *The North American Indian.* (Norwood, Mass.: The Plimpton Press, 1913).
3. Homer G. Barnett, *The Coast Salish of British Columbia,* University of Oregon Monographs, Studies in Anthropology no. 4. (Eugene, Oregon: University of Oregon, 1955).
4. Barbara Lane, "A Comparative and Analytic Study of Some Aspects of Northwest Coast Religion" (Ph.D. diss., University of Washington, Seattle, 1953).
5. Frank Morrison, ed., "[Camas] Indian Native Culture" (Paper based on panel discussion involving Morrison and three Camas Indians held at meeting of United Nations Society, Chemainus, B.C., 19 November 1952).

To reconstruct the past accurately is, of course, a very difficult task. Fortunately, for my purposes there is no necessity to try to picture the early Camas culture in minute detail. If the fundamental values that were the motive force for home and village and tribal life and that welded the culture into a working whole can be illuminated, then we have clues to understanding at least some of the values of the present—a present so close to the past that it is like a transparency laid over a map. Broad outlines should suffice to provide these clues and to show us how it was that the individuals of this society were at one time able to live successfully and even with wealth and leisure on their rivers and shores, with the wild Northwest forests at their back door.

LOCATION AND TERRAIN

The Coast Salish Indians form a cultural continuum from the north end of the Strait of Georgia to the southern end of Puget Sound or beyond. Within this large related group are numerous tribes, some more closely related linguistically than others; and within the tribes are the bands, the name given to the small groups of households constituting villages, and found at the mouths of the rivers of any size, on both the eastern shore of Vancouver Island and the mainland.

The Camas Band may be identified first of all as the inhabitants of a group of villages located between the site of the town and the bay, a distance of about eight miles by road today. Aboriginally, these villages were not a single band; each bore its own name. Though there may have been twelve of them at one time, today there are seven distinguishable village locales, still retaining individual names. However, because of their nearness and community of interests and kinship, they attained long ago an unusual unity, and as early as 1886 the "Indian Agent" was dealing with them as with one group, meeting with them in a common council.

The Camas Band, then, is a convenient way—and today an administratively accurate way—to refer to the Indians of seven closely related villages occupying the aboriginal sites and isolated to an extent by the surrounding reserve of 5,723 acres.

The Camas Band, however, is not the only band within the larger tribe. Anthropologists have not always agreed as to the exact extent of the group to which the common name should refer. But whether the tribe included groups on the Canadian mainland or was confined to a smaller area on Vancouver Island —and embracing also some of the Gulf Islands—the important point is that its members had friendly contacts with closely related bands up and down the coast. They could not communicate with the Nootka to the west and were at odds with the Comox, the northernmost Salish, adjoining the Kwakiutl territory; but their linguistic affinities enabled them to travel and to arrange alliances with groups to the north, to the south, on the Gulf Islands, and on the mainland.

Water travel was an essential part of their existence; water the most important environmental factor in their lives. Habitations up and down these coastal areas were on the shores or near the mouths of the rivers that flowed down from the densely forested inland mountains. An irregular coastline and nearby islands in the calm waters of the strait made for a maximum of shore, where clams, mollusks, and waterfowl abounded. Herring, seal, porpoise, and halibut were also plentiful; but salmon was the staple food, so abundant in Camas Bay that "up until almost the end of the nineteenth century their leaping and splashing . . . was a roar which could be heard a mile away."[6]

The villages at the scattered river mouths were but small clusters of large plank dwellings lining the shore, perhaps with no more than from one to five houses in each cluster. In the spring many of them appeared dismantled; their owners had taken down the wall planks and carried them off to make shelters at the spring camping sites. For life was a matter of camping and moving, throughout the spring and fall months, in a recurring seasonal pattern: in March to an island in the Strait for herring, then back to the villages till May, when the much prized camas root was ready for digging on the islands; in June,

6. From a historical article by E. Blanche Norcross in local newspaper, 6 June 1957.

off again, this time to the Fraser River across the Strait, for the sock-eye and the huckleberries, then back to the villages in September, with the salmon dried and the dog salmon about ready to run in the rivers; from November to March, no traveling about, no working—this was the time for the winter ceremonies in the permanent villages.

Elk and deer were hunted occasionally, but by and large it was the water and not the land that provided sustenance, and provided it in great abundance. From the land came the cedar for canoes and houses and the cedar bark for clothing. The forests, like the water, were prodigal. Rain fell liberally throughout the year; the climate was mild.

If they were placed on a relief map, the permanent winter villages of these coastal Indians would appear as the merest spots, lost against the spaces, the heights, the wildness of the Northwest terrain. But the map would be overlaid and occasionally crisscrossed with the water routes, showing how the small bands of one tribe traversed annually the same widespread territory and how members of different tribes came together occasionally at favorable bargaining points.

This, then, in broad outline, is the geographical setting. In the early days before the White man, as now, the Northwest Coast was a land of great beauty, laid out on an immense scale. Mountains rise from the water; lakes and bays and straits extend for miles; the trees of the deep, thick forests are those giants, the cedar and the Douglas fir.

As we shall see, it was here, under these trees and on these lake shores, that the individual Indian found the spirit power that befriended him throughout his life and helped him make his way.

KINSHIP SYSTEM

A network of relatives could be depended on for help as well. But as in the case of all peoples who reckon descent bilaterally, the kinship group of the Camas Indian was literally a network —never one solid large clan group, capable of collective action. Maternal aunts, uncles, grandmothers, and in-laws were scattered up and down the coast, and they could be useful in many ways in a culture lacking any formal social or political confederations and aboriginally characterized by considerable inter- and intra-group distrust and conflict. This kinship structure, embodying a network of valued relationships, is one of the important keystones of the culture, as important as the terrain itself, spotted with camp sites and fishing locations. A consideration of the kinship system leads us into all the closely interlinked features of the economic life and social organization, as well as the religious life and concepts and values revolving around status.

Though the system of descent and inheritance was bilateral, there was some preference for the patrilineal, and residence was generally patrilocal, though there were many exceptions to this rule. In terms of the actual structure of the households, this means that the inhabitants of a village (the one to five large plank dwellings clustered together on the river banks) were a large extended family, consisting of a man and his sons and their children, as well as brothers and paternal cousins and their wives; occasionally, sons-in-law might also be included. Not infrequently, too, there were plural wives, particularly for the headmen—those eldest sons who nominally owned the land and were looked to for guidance and protection.

Wives were usually sought outside the village, though there were no taboos against marriage of kin as nearly related as third cousins, and such marriages did take place within the village group. But alliances with distant villages, through marriage, were favored, because of the protection and hospitality they might afford outside of the local group; and plural wives—from different villages—made sense in a culture where the aim and basis of marriage was the gaining of as many desirable social connections as possible.

A "village," of course, began with one large dwelling. These rough plank houses, forty feet or more wide and seventy feet or more long, were built to shelter four or more separate, but closely related, families: each had its own corner and its own fire on the earth floor and owned the house planks in its section of the building. As the families grew and sons and brothers needed more space, additional plank houses were erected, through the joint efforts of all. Thus gradually groups of brothers and male cousins became the founders of such clusters of villages as at Camas Bay. Primogeniture was the rule, though daughters did occasionally inherit important property, and personal qualifications also entered in, when decisions were made as to property inheritance.

Such a system engendered certain frictions and difficulties, and a consideration of how some of these were resolved will illuminate further the role of the scattered kin group. Difficulties could arise not only in connection with the crowded extended household living, with its very informal organization, but also in connection with inheritance, under a system in which wealth was of central importance. A man who was dissatisfied with his household conditions or with the leadership of the headman could seek living quarters with maternal relatives; this was considered a very natural procedure. Likewise, the youngest son of a youngest son, who might find himself with almost no property, even though a direct descendant of one of the noble headmen, might choose to live in the village of his bride and might be welcomed there because of his connections.

The significant point for us here is that relatives were *used*; none were cast off because of membership on the mother's side; those at a distance were seen, visited, "helped"; their names, and the exact statuses belonging to these names, were known and passed on to children bilaterally; and a classificatory system of terminology embraced them all, indicating the common functions, the common status. Grandparents on both sides were called by a single term, including also grandparents' siblings. Cousins were equated with brothers and sisters, and there were no distinctions made between parents' siblings.

Relatives on both sides of the family were of a help in a culture where "gift giving" was an all-important mechanism, pervading the whole structure of the society. Not only were gifts given as payment for work, but they were an indispensable part of the public ceremonies surrounding every life crisis; they were used as mechanisms for eradicating shame and saving face; and of course at the great intervillage potlatches, reaching their most extravagant heights after the White man had introduced changes in the economy, privilege and prestige were demonstrated through giving away of blankets, food, canoes. Accumulation of goods for the purpose of distributing them, always to one's own profit in prestige, underlay the whole economic activity of Salish life and provided the incentive for work.

Relatives on the mother's as well as the father's side helped in these accumulations; they were expected to give "loans" to an individual when he needed help in amassing enough goods for a potlatch. Relatives were indispensable in the whole system of lending and repayment that made potlatching possible.

The most actively cooperating group of relatives, of course, was that constituting the household, or households, in the village. United by close blood kinship, common traditions, economic necessity, and a shared prestige, this village group formed the basic social unit in Salish life. There was no other social grouping that superseded it; no other organized social institutions to which an individual could have recourse.

SOCIAL ORGANIZATION AND STATUS

A description of the functioning of the household group becomes a description, largely, of the status system which upheld the whole structure. At the head of each household was the headman who, as we have said, was the nominal owner of the important economic resources used by his group—the fishing and hunting sites, the gathering grounds, and important pieces of equipment and furnishings. Likewise he had control of the use of the inherited family ceremonial privileges and displays—the special masks, or rattles, or songs that could be displayed at public ceremonies. Under the rule of primogeniture, he had inherited the nominal control of this wealth and privilege and would pass it on to his eldest son.

He lived, however, in the same house with his close kin; and though he belonged to the group of "aristocrats" (revered elder sons, wise leaders), no wide gulf separated him from his housemates of lesser rank. All of them had an inalienable right to the use of the various properties, and the headman's ownership was more in the nature of trusteeship. Furthermore, he had to earn the cooperation and loyalty of his family through demonstration of his ability to hold title to the wealth. He had to prove his wisdom and give constant evidence of his generosity. He had no true political power. As a matter of fact, others might be looked to for leadership in war pursuits—others who had special fighting powers.

Life in one of the big households can be pictured as one which was filled, during the winter months, with ceremonies and dances at which the headman, with the cooperation of his housemates, lavishly entertained and bestowed gifts upon others outside of his family for the purpose of validating his rights to greater and greater privileges, such as the ownership of wealth and the adoption of names of high status. There were also many occasions when the headman entertained and feasted his own extended family.

Under this system of inheritance of wealth and privilege, there was probably little opportunity for a "commoner" to climb into a top position. What social status a common man could lay claim to was mainly that as member of a great house, contributing to and sharing in its various forms of prestige and receiving the favors the leader could and did bestow.

Cooperation, then, was the rule in the big households. Blood kinship united the headman with his most insignificant second cousin; all traced their descent from a common ancestor; all lived under the same roof, on the same earth floor, without invidious distinctions. The only despised men were slaves, who were indeed in a class apart—outsiders, captured from an enemy tribe—and the "worthless," lazy men who constituted a small lower class of individuals who, as Suttles suggests,[7] had "lost their history" and their knowledge of good conduct.

7. Wayne Suttles, "Private Knowledge, Morality, and Social Classes among the Coast Salish," *American Anthropologist* 9 (June 1958): 501.

Furthermore, economic cooperation was essential to obtain certain of the necessary articles for living, in this culture of specialized skills. Not every man knew how to make canoes, or tan hides, or make weapons or household utensils. These were individual prerogatives, vouchsafed by guardian spirit power. Though in general there were men's tasks and women's tasks, still the individual was privileged to devote his major energies to his special skill, and the necessary goods of life were obtained through constant exchange within the village. Cooperation was required, too, in such enterprises as raising the roof beams or setting in the large upright posts of a new Big House.

Debts were inherited and paid by the whole family group; in the case of a murder committed by one member, the entire extended family was held collectively responsible and might become involved in bloodshed if a feud developed. Intermarriage was possible between those who were directly descended from the headman and those whose relation to him might be very attenuated. These were the privileges and the fruits of cooperation, under a system that contained schismatic tendencies in the simple fact that great wealth—essential for high rank—was not obtainable by all.

There was a further condition that operated to negate somewhat the social inequalities inherent in the system. Each man's status was his own and not exactly that of any other man; there was no clear dividing line between an aristocrat and a commoner. This, of course, was the result of a system in which order of birth determined right to inherit wealth, and so rank within a family.

Furthermore, status was identifiable with a name, and names of individuals were kept alive, the right to them inherited, and all their attributes kept in the public eye. Nothing demonstrates this more clearly than the ceremonial procedure of the potlatch, where gifts were allocated always according to the rank of the guests, and there was always a careful adherence to order of rank in calling the names.

Great names were few, but because of the individual rank inherent in each name, it was an honor to be able to assume one just a step higher, even though it might not be a great one. This could be done by industrious commoners who could accumulate enough food and gifts to make a small public demonstration of generosity, thus validating claim to the name. Often a great potlatch consisted not only of the central event—the validation claims of the headman, the display of his inherited ceremonial masks or rattles and dances, and the ostentatious allocation of gifts—but also a series of minor individual distributions made by the lesser relatives. Sometimes the headman himself conferred new names upon certain of his henchmen, just as it was his responsibility to do so for his children, to advance them in status.

Within this system, tremendous rivalry existed among the high-ranking headmen at the intervillage potlatches, each aiming to outdo the other, and each one highly conscious of his rank and open to insult if the gifts he received there in the public gathering were out of proportion to his own concept of his prestige. The donor must attempt, also, to allocate gifts in accordance with the recipient's ability to return more than he was given. Camas Indians state that it was the Camas custom to return double the amount. No gift could be refused, regardless of its great size. No headman would open himself to the shame inherent in any hint that he could not return the gift in double amount. If he had no extra resources at the time, then began the calling in of "loans" made to relatives and friends, and the asking of additional "help"—all to be repaid later. Under this system of intense rivalry for display of prestige, quarreling developed that sometimes led to violence and death, followed by revenge and warfare between the tribes involved. Marian Smith, in her study of the Salish Indians at Puyallup, Washington, found that there, too, the large intervillage potlatch meetings threatened violence. However, she pointed out that the distribution of property and exchange of gifts in itself operated as a mechanism for establishing temporary friendliness and that the prestige of the headmen depended somewhat upon their skill in keeping their adherents under control at these occasions. Furthermore, it was felt that the success of the gambling games, which were always played at these festivities, not only at Puyallup but all up and down the coast, depended upon participants and onlookers keeping their minds free of ill will.[8]

Throughout Coast Salish society, the ceremonial phraseology used by the potlatch donors embraced the concept of "thanks for coming." Generosity, help, friendliness, giving—these were the accepted social formulations of the potlatch.

In this society, then, where pride and ambition were strong motive forces, there were numerous mechanisms operating in compensatory fashion to make cooperation possible within the large competitive framework and to assure for each individual a share of prestige.

SPIRIT POWER

Little mention has been made, so far, of the spirit power concept. Actually, it is of crucial pertinence in any discussion of the pride and prestige dynamics of Salish culture. Belief in the presence and power of spirit forces sustained the individual, directed his occupational pursuits, and furnished him with a unique possession which he could display at winter ceremonies in the shape of a dance, a cry, a song, and so find release for himself and strength in the eyes of his people.

Central to the concept of spirit power was the belief that the animal world and the natural world were infused with supernatural powers whose aid and direction human beings could seek, through the vision quest. Rigorous preparation for encounter with the animal or other creature which was to direct the choice of occupation and become one's own helper began in childhood, and during puberty it was expected that each individual, girl as well as boy, should make the attempt. No one could expect to achieve great success without a spirit helper. For

---

8. Marian Smith, "The Puyallup of Washington," in *Acculturation in Seven Indian Tribes*, ed. Ralph Linton (New York: Appleton-Century-Crofts, 1940), pp. 19–20.

fishing, hunting, doctoring, and canoe-making supernatural help was deemed especially important. Women sought lesser spirits, perhaps those that might grant them aid in domestic proficiency.

"Aid" was conceived of as power to succeed in the occupation represented by the spirit; and tangible evidence of help was given in the bestowal of a unique "song" unlike that bestowed upon any other individual, various incantations or formulas to use while at work, the use of the "cry" of the animal, and specifications for painting the face. In some cases, this spirit also bestowed dancing power, as will be explained below.

The actual encounter with the animal who was to bestow the power usually took place in the woods, under some unusual circumstance. Later, at home, the indispensable encounter with the spirit and the bestowal of power took place in a dream, in such a way that the dreamer knew he had found the spirit that was to be his helper throughout life, nontransferable—unless he were a shaman—and leaving him only as he weakened in old age. Tremendous secrecy must surround the encounter with the spirit. Indeed, the young person was taught that it might leave him if he divulged his experience in any way; and so private a matter it was that even family members did not always know just which of their young people had acquired power.

It can be seen that belief in the ability of anyone to secure a unique spirit helper—even though it might be one of the weaker spirits—must have acted as a tremendous bolster to confidence and must have contributed something to the individual's sense of having a personal status unlike anyone else's.

Of course, it did not work out in practice that a commoner could dream "wealth power" or even canoe power and be assured of climbing to the top. Undoubtedly individuals were taught many of the necessary skills of a trade by their relatives, and thus became somewhat predisposed to dream of a certain animal spirit, who could bestow on them the power to achieve a skill they were already well on the way toward achieving. A commoner who dreamed "wealth power" lacked the material advantages to help him profit from the dream, as a headman might. Nevertheless, the idea was current that a man could raise his status through industry and through capitalizing on the special abilities that had been vouchsafed him by his guardian spirit, and undoubtedly this occasionally happened.

It is for this reason that Ruth Benedict has characterized the Salish as "individualists," in contrast to Kwakiutls further north, where hereditary privileges were more rigidly stressed.[9]

SPIRIT DANCING

The spirit power concept related not only to occupations, but to dancing in the winter ceremonies. It was believed that anyone who had been truly possessed by a spirit carried this spirit within him, more or less inactive, until winter came around. At that time the power began to make itself felt, and to "want out." The signs of this possession were a general spirit lassitude, characterized by loss of appetite, pains in the chest and side, involuntary singing during sleep, and crying spells. It was believed that this condition could be relieved only by singing and dancing. Night after night during the winter months, the Big Houses were filled with friends and relatives called to watch the initiation of a new dancer, and the dancing performances of those who had already been initiated and were seeking outlet for the powers welling up in them.

"Initiation" as a dancer was essential, though there was actually no organized society for the novice to enter. The initiation procedure was an extended and arduous one, paralleling in some respects the private and personal spirit encounter the individual was assumed to have had earlier. Through arrangement by the parents, the ailing young person was "seized" by several older people, who became his attendants for four days as they attempted to put him into a trance state and to help the "song" come out of him. He might be beaten, his breath blown back into his body, or his head held under water, until he became limp. He was then kept under cover on the bed

---

9. Ruth Benedict, *Patterns of Culture* (Boston: Houghton Mifflin Company, 1934), pp. 226–27.

platform in one curtained-off corner of the Big House. His attendants gave him very little to eat or drink, kept up a constant drumming, rattling, and singing, and attempted to detect sounds—cries or sobs—coming from him that might be interpreted as his song taking shape. Other ritual procedures were carried out until the fourth day, by which time the initiate had found his song and dance. He was then led out to the woods by a rope around his waist for a period of vigorous running, walking, and swimming, his face painted in the requisite fashion by a ritualist. Upon his return, on the night of the fourth day, he donned the wool headdress of the initiate; and before the assembled spectators drumming on the planks of the house, he performed for the first time his own spirit dance. Then came the necessary distribution of gifts by his parents, both to the attendants who had "helped" and to the spectators.

The novice was then privileged to dance each night of the dancing season, which lasted from November to March or April. During this first season he was, however, subject to numerous taboos and was expected to break out at times in uncontrolled frenzies when he was seized by his power. At such times attendants took hold of the rope which had been left around his waist and conducted him as he danced and sang from house to house. He wore his face paint throughout the entire season.

During the season following his initiation, he became a full member, no longer using the goat's wool headdress, but often adopting items of costume that suggested the spirit animating his song. Each night during the winter ceremonies he could take his place in the Big House with all the other initiated dancers and rise to dance alone when he felt his spirit possessing him. Nondancers sat and watched, beating on the planks with sticks ringed with two bands of deer hoof rattles. Dancers tied deer hoof rattles around their ankles. There in the midst of this din, by the light of the fires on the earth floor, the dancers performed their animated, rhythmic, shuffling steps and intoned their monotonous chants called "songs." When dawn broke, it was time for the feast that ended the ceremony.

The song welling up in the initiate was never the song his

"occupational" spirit had given him, though the animal animating both of them might be the same one. The purposes of the winter dance ceremonies were completely apart from those of the occupational spirit-seeking; sometimes an individual had one spirit for his occupational helper and another for his dance spirit. However that might be, the two songs had to be entirely separate, even though theoretically there was a complex linkage in the basic concept that a true spirit possession lay at the base of the illness seizing the young initiate.

As Barbara Lane points out,[10] it was quite possible that young people were sometimes initiated and helped to find dancing songs, when actually they had not previously been possessed by a spirit. Perhaps an ordinary illness had been mistakenly identified as spirit lassitude. Indeed, the true spirit encounter was such a personal affair and was kept so secret, that even close relatives could have no certainty that it had taken place for one of their family members. This fact has a bearing on the later, post-contact practice of sometimes inducting, with conscious intent, young people who did not possess power—a practice which will be discussed more fully in the section on contemporary practices.

Spirit dancing served a number of functions. The literature contains numerous accounts of "cures" in post-contact times, attested to by informants. That such cures took place in pre-contact times also seems highly probable and in keeping with current psychological theory that recognizes the benefits of emotional expression. Not only did the singing and dancing demand vigorous bodily expression, but it gave the dancer mastery of a new skill plus the opportunity to win approval and admiration from the whole community—all of which could well be conducive to psychological well-being.

Barnett suggests, also, that the dancing and the opportunity to give vent to frenzied seizures may have provided a healthy outlet for the adolescent facing alone his encounters with the supernatural. "Brooding over their experiences, which were

10. Lane, "Northwest Coast Religion," p. 31.

mysterious and often terrifying, adolescents must have felt an inward turmoil that at times demanded uncontrolled expression. There had to be some outlet, and the culture sanctioned one in the periodic spirit demonstrations in the winter time. These were ecstatic releases, scarcely held in check through critical situations during the rest of the year." [11]

There was also the simple function of entertainment. During the winter months when there was little necessity for work, in this culture of abundance, the winter ceremonies provided a colorful and exciting occupation. And by feasting the guests in his house, the headman added further to his prestige.

OTHER USES OF THE SUPERNATURAL

Supernatural forces sometimes worked for ill, as well as for good, according to Camas belief. An individual was perhaps never completely free of the fear that some malevolent magic was being worked upon him through the powers of an evil shaman. An enemy could pay a malicious shaman to "shoot" an object such as a small bone into a victim and in this way cause illness; or the shaman could send one of his spirits into a victim, to make him ill, or could steal his soul and hide it away. The shaman could and did bring about cures as well as sickness, and some were relied upon for curing, but all were held in awe because of their potentially evil powers.

According to Barbara Lane, the Indian found comprehensible reasons for the shaman's evil doing. He considered that the shaman might be a "mean" or jealous person, or might have acquired a spirit power that was "bad" and made him kill without the shaman's conscious intent.[12] Nor was the Indian without recourse when a shaman was suspected of evil doing. Aboriginally, the shaman might be murdered and a blood feud thus initiated, or another shaman might be hired to kill him through use of his own methods.

Other means were available, too, for coping with the many

11. Barnett, *Coast Salish*, p. 146.
12. Lane, "Northwest Coast Religion," p. 46.

supernatural dangers feared in Camas life, such as the wandering away of a soul, lured by the ghosts of the recent dead, or frightened away by a sudden accident; or infraction of taboos such as that against association with a menstruating woman.

There were several different kinds of religious functionaries besides the regular shaman, who could be employed to ease the way through the life crises and to help the individual through supernatural dangers. The ritualist knew secret formulas to be used at life crisis rites, and had many varied functions. He could both kill and cure, like the shaman; he could ease a difficult birth and lift puberty taboos; he could instruct parents of newborn twins in the rites necessary to purge themselves after such an unfortunate birth; he knew love magic and hunting magic; he could cleanse and purify a house after a funeral. His formulas and acts, jealously guarded, were inherited family lore. The seer—who was usually a woman—could be employed to look into the future and ward off evil mischances that might be impending. And the medium could be hired to contact dead relatives, who could give information as to the causes of their death.

It is difficult to reconstruct such a tenuous thing as the atmosphere or climate of feeling that must have pervaded Camas life, as a result of the belief in evil powers, mischances, and supernatural dangers. Marian Smith believes that the Salish of Puyallup lived in an atmosphere of suspicion and constant surveillance due to the belief that the evil powers of other people were constantly at work to bring about accidents and mischances; and as we have already seen, she links the gift-giving mechanism of the society not only with the economic need for fluidity of goods, but also with the need to clear away suspicion and lay the foundations for good will and friendship.[13] Further, she suggests that when army officials and missionaries began to bring pressures for giving up communal living in the big houses, the move to single-family dwellings was easily made, and provided welcome relief from the strains and suspicions of close social contact.[14]

13. Smith, "Puyallup," pp. 14–15.
14. Ibid., p. 30.

Wayne Suttles, in his study of the Lummi Salish group across the Strait in Washington, also reports the presence of a belief that hostile forces were constantly at work: "Some informants, at least, have been very quick to attribute both illnesses and deaths to supernatural causes, or to natural causes resulting from someone's hostility." [15]

Barnett, also, describes the life of the Salish groups of Vancouver Island and the Canadian mainland as characterized by distrust, in both intergroup and intervillage relations. He appears to be referring mainly, however, to the unfriendly relations existing between tribes, and describes the night raids that took place between villages aboriginally. The initial provocation for these was sometimes merely the desire of a novice warrior to test the strength of his "war power" spirit; sometimes a plundering expedition was undertaken to relieve grief over death of a near relative. Heads and slaves and other plunder were taken.[16]

It is known that the Camas Indians were subject to depredations from the northern Kwakiutls and that they made at least one retaliatory raid, which took place a few years previous to 1850 at one of the bays near their own locality. Curtis describes the band as more warlike than the average Salish tribe and tells of early chiefs who were professional fighting men and greatly feared because of their tendency to "run amuck." [17] There are other numerous bloodthirsty accounts of assassinations and murders that took place in the early half of the nineteenth century.[18]

That there were enmities, and that they found expression both in malevolent magic and in murder, is true. But for the malevolence, there were ritual counter-charms; for murder, there was the blood-feuding system of revenge. Also, murder could be set right through payment; and it was expected that

---

15. Wayne Suttles, "Post-Contact Culture Change among the Lummi Indians," *British Columbia Historical Quarterly* 18 (January-April 1954): 94.
16. Barnett, *Coast Salish,* pp. 267–71.
17. Curtis, *Salishan Tribes,* pp. 32–35.
18. From a historical article by the Reverend Father Francis in local newspaper, 19 April 1928.

all conflicts—such as fights and insults—regardless of whether murder was involved, would be followed by exchange of goods in order to restore friendship. Indeed, if serious conflicts were witnessed by others, it was obligatory to call the witnesses and distribute gifts, to wipe out the shame.

In short, there were methods for dealing with dangers, both natural and supernatural. As Barbara Lane expressed it, the Camas had worked out a system of checks and balances. For every problem there was a solution, indicating "an ordering and integration of cultural material into a rather well organized system." [19]

LIFE AFTER DEATH

Did religious belief in a land of the dead or in immortality play any part in this ordering and integrating? It seems unlikely that there was any concept of a deity or of other worlds which functioned as significantly for the Camas as the concept of supernatural aid from the guardian spirit. Boas reports that all the Salish tribes believed in a deity called "The Great Transformer," and that in post-contact times this deity was often identified with Jesus.[20] In "[Camas] Indian Native Culture," one Great Spirit is identified as "The All-Powerful One," who created and placed in the Camas valley the full-grown man who became the ancestor of the tribe. The Indians explain that this Spirit was to be respected but not worshiped:

> We were taught to respect him and to use the blessings he sent, but not to spoil or waste his creations. Our ancestors did not exactly worship the Great Spirit, but rather respected him above all else.... Supplications or prayers were offered for success in all important enterprises. These were generally addressed to mediators, like for instance, the Thunderbird or some other bird or animal spirits—guardians of which there were many who lived in the unseen

---

19. Lane, "Northwest Coast Religion," p. 92.
20. Franz Boas, "Second General Report," p. 579. An anecdote told to me by one of my own informants verifies this.

places—something like our Christian Saints—each having special powers to help us get certain things we wanted.[21]

Beliefs about life after death were vague and ill-defined. As the above Indian informants expressed it:

> When at sunset the sky was sometimes filled with red clouds, the Indians thought that that was a sign that one of their people had died, and they therefore went around visiting to find out who it was, that they might bring help to the relative. The hooting of owls was also thought of as the voices of spirit people, for our ancestors believed that the souls of the departed dwelt for a time in the air above their former homes, watching to see what their living relatives would do to their honour.... The early [Camas] Indians destroyed the personal possessions of their dead and burned food for them. It was believed that by this means what they had about them during life would become available for their use in the unknown life to which they had passed.[22]

There was some fear of the dead when they became "ghosts," and of their power to lure off the souls of the living; but there was no concept of or fear of any kind of hell filled with punishments. Nor, on the other hand, was there a heaven filled with rewards. There seemed to be some belief in the possibility of reincarnation, either in animal form or human form—that is, an ancestor might come to life again in a child.

The emphasis in Camas thought was on life in this world. What had to be settled, must be settled here. It was so that their names and all the status associated with them might live on this earth that elderly people went to great pains to give great naming ceremonies for their grandchildren. It might even be postulated that it was partly because of the importance of earthly life, as against life after death, that children were so welcomed and loved. Devereux has suggested, that "there may exist a functional relationship between a lack of deep belief in true personal immortality, and kindness and respect toward children."[23]

21. Morrison, "Native Culture."
22. Ibid.
23. George Devereux, "Status, Socialization, and Interpersonal Relations of Mohave Children," *Psychiatry* 13 (November 1950): 492.

Just how the lives of children were affected by Camas belief will emerge as we look now at the round of daily living in the big households and consider the cycle of growth from infancy to old age.

THE CYCLE OF LIFE

The Big House was a rough, shed-like structure, with an earthen floor. It had no windows. Light and air came through the two doors—in the front and rear walls—and through the cracks. Smoke from the fires, which were built on the earth floor, found its way out through holes in the roof. The early Catholic missionaries called these great drafty dwellings "camps," [24] and they must indeed have had a camp-like appearance to the White settlers.

Upon entering, one's impression must have been of a great many objects not only hanging above the fires on drying racks, but piled around the sides against the walls, on and under the sleeping platform which was built at a height of about three feet from the ground. There was wood to be stored; there were tools, utensils, the weaving equipment of the women; the clothing of cedar bark and skins; the ceremonial objects. Only the central floor space was unobstructed. A statement in "[Camas] Indian Native Culture" provides some evidence that a great many odds and ends of things were saved and stored for future use, but also emphasizes an attempt at neatness:

Everything inside the house must be kept clean and in order, and outside, too. The elder would order someone of the family to pick up trash, take and throw it in the river, to be carried away by the sea. But they must first carefully pick out and save all scraps of useful things, like dog or mountain goat hair, cedar bark, and limestone, which was used for making things white. They must save every article that was made of something that never must be wasted.[25]

24. From a scrapbook kept by a Catholic nun in the locality.
25. Morrison, "Native Culture."

There was very seldom any attempt to beautify either the exterior or interior. After all, these "permanent" dwellings were permanent only for the winter months, and at least some of them were partially dismantled each year for the summer trips to the fishing and berrying locations. Mats woven of rushes were hung on the inside walls to help keep out drafts, and occasionally there was some rough carving of house posts, but this was rare and of little significance as one of the ceremonial "privileges." [26]

Infancy and Childhood

The arrival of a new baby in one of these Big Houses was an event which was generally welcomed. Infanticide was not practiced. If a poor family found itself with too many children to care for, there were always close relatives who would take a child or two to bring up. Ritualism and taboos for the parents were associated with the birth, as with other important life crises. And the infant himself provided the occasion for public ceremony only four days after the birth, when women were invited in for both food and gifts.

The first few months of his life—probably six months to a year—were spent on a cradle board, which his mother carried in her arms when she took him with her on her errands outside of the house. Inside the house the cradle might be hung from a cedar branch put up for the purpose. The mother could keep it rocking by means of a cord attached to her foot, which she could tap as she sat weaving.

The cradle was not only for the baby's comfort and the mother's convenience. The infant was bound in it in such a way that pressure was brought against his forehead, by means of a cedar bark pad, for the purpose of giving him a head-flattened appearance that was considered aesthetically desirable. Apparently the infant raised no objections to this procedure. In fact, parents believed that it was comfortable and that the shad-

---

26. I saw such a carved post in an abandoned Big House of post-contact times, in one of the Camas villages. The lower beam of the sleeping platform, lying horizontal on the ground, was carved in a thunderbird design.

ing of the cedar bark pad, as it fell over the eyes, was conducive to sleep.

Other steps, too, were taken to insure that the child would grow up with a well-shaped and ornamented body. His limbs, shoulders, and hips might be rubbed and squeezed in the desired directions; and the septum of the nose and lobe and helix of the ear were pierced shortly after birth, so that ornaments could be worn later.

If Underhill's findings for the Salish Indians of the Oregon and Washington coasts are applicable to the Camas groups of Vancouver Island, then we can assume that efforts were made to keep the baby happy by learning his likes and dislikes, and by keeping him away from people who were ill; parents were warned not to quarrel or even think unkind thoughts around a baby, if they wanted him to remain well. It was believed that if the baby did not like his life on earth, he could choose to go back to babyland. He was nursed whenever he cried and was taken out of his cradle daily for bathing and massage.[27] Boas reported that among the Songish—a group closely related to the Camas—a husband might beat his wife if the child cried.[28]

The cradle was left behind after about a year, and the infant's induction into the ceremonial life so important to his tribe was begun in earnest. His first naming ceremony was held when he was about a year old, at which time a grandparent from either side of the family usually conferred upon the child his own name—with the wish to keep it alive—and of course made a donation of goods to the assembled guests. And even while he was quite a small child, his parents, or his grandparents and uncles, would begin involving him in the indispensable economic and prestige transactions of ceremonies and potlatches, putting him forward and announcing that certain of the gifts

27. Ruth Underhill, *Indians of the Pacific Northwest,* Education Division of the United States Office of Indian Affairs, Indian Life and Customs, no. 5 (Washington: Government Printing Office, 1944), pp. 128–31.
28. Boas, "Second General Report," p. 574.

were being bestowed in his name. Only in this way could his name begin to accumulate prestige.

Certain of the ceremonies and rites were not open to the young child, however. He was kept away from funerals in order that he might be protected from the contamination and supernatural dangers believed to emanate from contact with the dead; and while he was a young child, he was not allowed to be present at the winter spirit dances, since his cries might disturb, or in his ignorance and innocence he might tend to mimic these very serious performances in his play. This does not mean that children were excluded from all aspects of the winter spirit dance initiations. They were expected to bring up the rear of the procession at those times when a new dancer, in a frenzied state of spirit possession, was led by his attendants through the village.

For neither the infant nor the child growing up in the Big House was the mother the all-important figure. There were many women to share the care of children—aunts, sometimes co-wives, and especially grandmothers. The latter figured very importantly in the child's life. The actual household arrangement was probably that a young groom brought his bride into the corner of the house where his parents were already set up. Not until one or two children were born did the young couple establish themselves in a separate area. The young woman giving birth to her first child was a girl of seventeen, eighteen, or younger, and her husband but little older.

It was the grandmother, not the mother, who wore the baby's umbilical cord around her neck, so that the child might be healthy. It was the grandmother—or grandfather—who bestowed a first name on the child. And it was the grandmother who became the caretaker when the child outgrew his cradle board and the mother was gone on long food-gathering trips. Grandparents were the storytellers, the teachers; they were the repositories of wisdom and knew how to instruct the children in the expected ways of behavior and in the rites and privileged ceremonial acts belonging to the family. They were the ones, too, who had time to play with children.

That the mother was not considered a person indispensable in the child's upbringing is evidenced, too, in the custom of disposition of the child in case of divorce. If he was an infant, he remained with the mother when she went back to her parents' home. Otherwise, it was expected that the child—male or female—would stay in the father's house since it was the father who was in a much better position to advance the child socially, by making expenditures in his behalf.

The child very early began to share in the rigors of living which were a part of the Salish code. With all the members of the Big House, he was routed out at dawn by the headman to bathe in the river, winter as well as summer—a custom continuing into the 1900s, according to a present-day Indian who recalled this in his own childhood experience. He was not allowed to be fussy with his food and was expected to obey his elders. The "lazy man" was the most derided figure in Salish culture, and children were expected to take a share in the general work. Boys learned the use of tools and weapons, and girls learned the weaving of mats and blankets. Both boys and girls were adept at catching and killing gulls, needed for their valuable down.

Mastery of physical skills was important, and children could usually swim by the age of eight. Barnett recounts an incident attesting to the shame a father (in a tribe closely related to the Camas) felt when his five- or six-year-old son, playing in a canoe, allowed it to be capsized by an older child. The boy could not swim, and was rescued by a woman. The father immediately presented gifts to the villagers, to save his face.[29]

In Salish life there was, of course, time for play for both adults and children, especially during the winter months. Children used shells as toys, and adults engaged in a great variety of games such as shinny, hoop-and-pole games, races, and the ever popular gambling games, which involved guessing which hands held the marked stick or bone. In fact, one of my informants, who lived in a Big House during his own childhood, recalled how

29. Barnett, *Coast Salish*, p. 279.

"Grandfather used to sit out there in front in that big cleared space and amuse us, with that game of passing the sticks and guessing."

Adolescence

With the approach of puberty, or even earlier, both boys and girls began the training that would enable them to secure spirit helpers. They were encouraged to make trips into the woods alone, to bathe and scrub themselves often. At the attainment of puberty, the boy was expected to make solitary and frequent trips into the woods over a period of as long as a year. He should swim, rub himself, fast, sleep alone on the shores of lakes, be unafraid at any unusual occurrence, and thus prepare himself for the encounter which was the prelude to his later meeting with his spirit in a dream. The belief was, according to "[Camas] Native Indian Culture," that "a man who never seeks restraint shall never know endurance and fortitude—never have visions of the spirit-world, nor understand the teachings of unseen wisdom." [30]

The girl, too, made these spirit quests at puberty, but was not expected to stay alone in the woods at night, nor to subject herself to such rigorous purification as the boy did. In fact, with the attainment of puberty she was carefully chaperoned. The girl's first menstruation was the occasion for one of the tribe's most ritualized observances, culminating in a great feast given by her family, with distribution of goods and costly exhibition of the family privileges. The extent and elaborateness of both the private and public rites varied in accord with the rank and wealth of the family.

The attractiveness of a girl for marriage embraced several concepts: physical attractiveness, which was enhanced by tattooing and by thinning the eyebrows and raising the hairline slightly on the forehead; industriousness and skill in household tasks; chastity and demure behavior.

A girl who had lost her chastity before marriage was con-

---

30. Morrison, "Native Culture."

sidered greatly cheapened and could not be "bought" in marriage. She could nevertheless marry, and her misdemeanor might be forgotten if she were reasonably faithful to her husband. If she was a headman's daughter, her seduction was considered as serious an offense as murder and required the same kind of settlement. Birth of an illegitimate child was also a matter for great shame and necessitated a presentation of gifts to the assembled guests, to clear the child's name.

Ready at fourteen or fifteen for marriage, the young girl hoped to be chosen by some wealthy family. Personal choice on her part played little or no part. The parents arranged the marriage and the daughter obeyed. Usually she would be married to someone roughly of her own rank. She was equipped with various household skills, but since she was still a very young girl and was moving into a household where older women were in charge and would continue to be in charge, marriage did not bring along with it demands for great responsibility. She had probably already acquired a spirit helper and might already have been initiated as a new dancer. In many cases she had learned from her mother and grandmother certain precious songs, rites, formulas, which were her inherited family possession. She may have received a second and a greater name. And if her family was of high rank, undoubtedly she would have been instructed in the ways of behavior and the code considered suitable for the best bred girls. This code may have included elements referred to by an Indian of one of the present Camas villages, speaking of his "high class" mother: she never sat on a chair, but "straight up," (on her heels); also she and her family treated slaves like sisters, unlike the people farther north, who treated them "bad."

The young man who was ready for marriage at sixteen or seventeen was equipped with numerous skills, though he was just at the threshold of his mature power. He had been learning ordinary wood, fishing, and hunting craft and lore from his father and grandfather, especially his grandfather. If one of his close relatives was a successful specialist at canoe-making, the boy had probably already learned a good deal about the craft himself; he might even have encountered an animal spirit who would be his guardian and guarantee him success in this same trade. However, no one knew of his spirit encounters, and indeed there was no requirement that he follow any occupation except one of his choice. Possibly he had already become a new dancer.

In addition to technical lore, he had also been taught the family ceremonial privileges, the family-owned myths and performances. For instance, if his father was one of the famous "swaihwe" dancers, owning one of the great "swaihwe" masks with bulging eyes and feathery plumes, the boy no doubt had already begun to learn some of the secrets connected with its use. He may have received a second name, and the rite celebrating his first kill had probably been performed—a rite initiated by his father or grandfather and involving the presence of guests who praised the accomplishment, admonished the young man to observe the old regulations, and were privileged to eat the meat.

There was no expectation that he should immediately assume the property negotiations which were the concerns of his elders. Indeed, at the time of marriage he was usually so young that he was without property, and so without status. The elaborate exchanges of gifts made by his parents and parents-in-law as a part of the marriage transactions—the "return" gift nominally made to him—were intended to give him a start as a property-manipulating, mature man.

Marriage and Maturity

The marriage followed established procedures involving choice of a girl by the boy's parents, "encampment" at her home by the groom and his father, "speakers" for the occasion, with an offering of gifts that were ritually refused many times, and then final acceptance of the gifts by the girl's family after they had apparently deliberated long. The actual ceremony involved eulogies by speakers for both sides before the assembled relatives and admonitions to the young couple who were seated upon piles of blankets. Feasting, distribution of blankets to speakers, and gifts to the young couple by the bride's father completed the rites for the time being. Actually, the marriage initiated a series of visits and gift exchanges between the in-law relatives.

The maximum of pomp and rite and gift exchange was carried on by the wealthy families. Common men who wanted wives secured them with much less ceremony. The parents chose a suitable girl, there was a meal together with friends, and a small exchange of property was made. Among the poor, the method of entering into the marital bond was simply through voluntary cohabitation.

The marriage could be terminated at will by either the husband or wife. The only formal requirement was a return of goods by the wife's relatives in an amount equal to that of the marriage gift. A man might disown his wife for such reasons as laziness, quarrelsomeness, fondness for gossip, or adultery or prostitution without his consent. The wife, on the other hand, might leave the husband if he lived dissolutely or improvidently. Divorce was easy, possibly because it was purely a family matter involving only disposition of children and matters of inheritance—all of which could be easily settled within the family group. Barnett believes that among the Camas, as well as the neighboring groups, marriages were fairly stable. Efforts to make them so were made by both sides of the family, and a daughter was not welcomed who returned home without her husband, unless she came because she was being mistreated.[31] When a spouse died, remarriage could take place as soon as the proper rites had been observed to guard against evil influences. The levirate and sororate were not a part of the system of obligations, but marriage of a deceased brother's wife, or or a deceased wife's sister, did sometimes occur.

The married woman occupied herself with women's work: gathering berries and clams, drying fish, preparing meals, and weaving great stores of goat hair blankets and rush mats for potlatch purposes. She learned the medicinal properties of herbs and could doctor ordinary ailments. Sometimes she was a ritualist who had inherited special formulas and acts from her mother, and so would be sought out for aid when twins were born, or to release a parent from taboos in connection with the birth of his first child, or to conduct the ritual for the pubescent

---

31. Barnett, *Coast Salish*, p. 194.

girl. Even the profession of shaman was open to her. Though she did not manipulate and inherit material property—except occasionally—she was an active owner of family songs and dances; she might be called upon to display her privileged dance with the shell rattle at crisis ceremonies; and she could be a spirit dancer as well, during the winter months. Thus, though her status was not as high as the man's, she had considerable autonomy. She was not bound irrevocably to her husband in marriage; she could develop skills valuable to the whole community; and as a spirit dancer she was a unique and self-sufficient individual.

The man, as he grew into maturity, occupied himself with hunting, fishing, building houses, and fetching in the large logs needed for fuel. His best efforts went in the directions in which he knew he would have special success, because of his spirit power. In the winter months he sang and danced and joined the gambling games, played to the noisy accompaniment of songs and drumming. Seeking greater names for himself and aiding his headman in the potlatch displays, he accumulated as much prestige for himself as possible and began to take responsibility for his children's names. His sons became his special charge. As the years accrued, so did his status, in this culture where privilege could be validated only through greater and greater displays of wealth. As a man left his youth behind, he entered upon the most important period of his life. A young man could have little status. An older man, on the other hand, was the wise man, the manipulator of property, the owner of great names.

We can surmise that the personal tie between parents and their children may not have been as intense and close as we experience it, in our nuclear family households. Where there were grandparents, aunts, uncles, and co-wives to share in the care of the many closely related children in the house, the parent-child bond may well have become attenuated—even the grandparent-child bond. Yet there is some evidence that children—all the children—were cherished and that, in spite of the authoritarian code of behavior, good will was the basic feeling conveyed. A diary record of one of the early Camas Indian Agents records a meeting held in his office on a day in May of 1913. Five Camas headmen, or "chiefs," were present, and five "councillors." They had come to protest what had been rumored as ill treatment of the children in one of the boarding schools. The record cites one of the chiefs as pleading that "the small children should not be punished severely. If the children are treated better, the Indians will feel very glad. . . . God made all the children. If the children are not treated right, God will punish whoever does them a wrong." [32] This, of course, was 1913, and the Indian speaker may have been voicing some of the defiance of the Whites current at that time, as well as his concern for children. Yet there is also the possibility that his words reflect attitudes established years earlier.

One might postulate further that the Camas Indian's lack of belief in a punishing or rewarding deity reflects a system of social relationships between adults and children similarly lacking in punishments or rewards. Walter B. Miller has suggested, in writing of the Fox Indians, that "the pantheon of any society can be seen as a projective system, whereby the essential features of the social organization of the projecting society are attributed to a group of supernatural beings, whose relations reflect those existing among the people themselves." [33]

Old Age and Death

As already indicated, status advanced with age and achievement among the Camas. Grandfathers were often the sponsors of important ceremonies; grandmothers knew the rituals and taboos and took charge in the important crisis rites such as the ceremonies for the pubescent girl. They were the overseers during the meat drying and other activities that demanded careful attention to regulations. Old people were the teachers, the caretakers and trainers of children, the knowledgeable ones who

---

32. From a MS. diary of the Indian Agent in local Indian agency files, 1913.
33. Walter B. Miller, "Two Concepts of Authority," *American Anthropologist* 62 (April 1955): 278–79.

there, because they hated to be away from their homes in the camps. By 1876 it was felt that the boarding school was needed to accommodate the "orphans"—those new members of the Indian society, the children of mixed blood, whose adventurous fathers had disappeared from the scene. The school was enlarged, renovated, and run as a home for the orphans.

That the early beginnings at schooling for the Indians were difficult is attested to by a notation of the agent in 1884 to the effect that no Indian school in the whole agency was successfully operating at that time. However, a Catholic day school for the Indian children was in operation in 1887, with thirty pupils enrolled. And in the 1890s, the Catholic boarding school on Kuper Island opened, to serve Indian children not only from the Camas Band but from many neighboring bands up and down the coast. This school, on an island five miles across the water in the Strait—a school which has affected the lives of Camas children over half a century now—had sixty-four pupils attending in September 1898, according to the agent's diary—just about half of its 1954 enrollment. The Protestant mission day school for Indian children, built on reserve land, was a smaller venture and did not open until 1911.

Not only the introduction of schooling met with resistances; many other attempts to bring in change encountered setbacks or complications. As early as 1864 the explorer Robert Brown, making an expedition into the general region under discussion here, left diary records attesting to the complaints the Indians were accumulating against the White men—complaints relative to the Whites taking the land, bringing in diseases, getting the women with child and then deserting them, driving away the deer and salmon—"and all this you did and now if we wish to buy a glass of fire water to keep our hearts up you will not allow us." [5]

The feeling about land ran strong. Only ten years after the Catholic church had been erected for the Indians—and a beauti-

---

5. Robert Brown, "Vancouver Island Exploring Expedition: June 7–20th, 1864" (typescript in Provincial Archives, Victoria, B.C.), entry for 9 June.

ful stone edifice it was—it was vacated, due to the incessant arguments of the Indians that it was on their land. Standing empty, it was attacked by wind and weather and made a ruin. A new church, meanwhile, was built a short distance away, just off the reserve.

Actually, complaints about land were not entirely unjustified. The Dominion and the Province were slow in working out a clear policy of compensation to the Indians of British Columbia for lands taken; issues were opened and reopened over the years; various Indian groups even presented their claims legally, including the Camas people, who sent a deputation to the king of England in 1906; commissions were set up to study the problems, and between 1913 and 1916 certain lands were cut off from reserves, where it was felt they were no longer needed, and others were added, but these were of lesser value than the lands that were taken away.[6]

Furthermore, the new system of land allotments to individual families led to constant disputes over boundaries between the Indians themselves, and sometimes between them and their White neighbors. In 1884 the Indian Agent wrote: "No murders of white men have taken place during the last three years.... But there are constantly a very large number of disputes about land and property of all kinds, and the Indian Office is often crowded for days together, while settling trouble of this kind."

It must be remembered that the Whites were settling down close to the Indians, on all sides. Not only were property boundaries sometimes hard to determine, but there were troubles due to the early lack of adequate fencing. The Indians complained that the White men arrived with cattle and hogs and let them roam and spoil their fields of potatoes. The settlers, on the other hand, by 1881 were complaining of the loss of many sheep, and supposed that the Indians were killing them. Back and forth the arguments continued. In 1907 the Indian Agent recorded that

---

6. See H. B. Hawthorn, C. S. Belshaw, and S. M. Jamieson, *The Indians of British Columbia: A Study of Contemporary Social Adjustment* (Berkeley and Los Angeles: University of California Press, 1958), pp. 48–57.

"Chief S—— says he feels very sad on account of the whitemen's impounding their stock, wants the Indian department to lay the matter before the municipal council.... We were told to be like white people and keep horses and cattle, we did so, but now we are always getting into troubles with them. Do you want to see us put our stock away and go back to our old customs?"

Farming, as an occupation and economic pursuit for the Indians, did not fare very well, for a number of reasons. As early as 1884 the agent noted that at harvest time the crops were neglected, because the Indians with their "wandering habits" and inability "to resist an offer of high wages, no matter at what future loss to their families" had taken off for the hop fields and canneries on the mainland, or over in the State of Washington. Furthermore, at this time high wage work became available to the Indians in Vancouver Island's new sawmill enterprises, in road work, and in clearing land for the White settlers. As one present-day Indian said, looking back on the early attempts to farm, "Maybe the Indians just lost interest, when jobs like logging and longshoring came along." Even in 1864, according to Robert Brown's diary,[7] the Indian was holding out for high wages, and it was difficult to secure his help as guide and canoe man, without paying the top wage of two dollars a day.

Money, the medium of exchange, brought wealth; and it must be remembered that wealth would buy prestige in the old Camas code. Furthermore, the trips to the canneries and hop fields, besides bringing in high wages, brought the opportunity for relatives and friends to meet, as they had of old during both the summer trips and the winter potlatch gatherings. Suttles cites a report by the agent across the Strait in the state of Washington describing the situation of the Lummi in 1895:

The Indians as a rule are not systematic farmers.... A large majority spend most of their time in their canoes, fishing, especially during the salmon season. In the summer they are absent most of the time picking berries. In early fall, with few exceptions, all, little and big, young and old, go to the hop fields where they meet old

7. Brown, "Expedition," entry for 10 June.

friends from all over the Sound and east of the mountains. Here they drink, gamble, and as they say, have a good time generally.[8]

Other developments, with the passage of time, contributed to the decline of farming. The necessity for growing oats for horses disappeared with the advent of the automobile. Furthermore, the land disputes and misunderstandings continued. Property was sometimes handed down when there had been no true ownership through possession of the location ticket; boundaries were unclear. It seems likely that what was true of the Lummi may have applied to the Camas as well, in the early 1900s. According to Suttles, the agent Buchanan reported in 1914 that "cases had been accumulating for years and that land had lain idle because its ownership could not be determined." [9]

Meanwhile, the records in the Camas Agency reveal that numerous convictions under the liquor clauses of the Indian Act continued; many council meetings were devoted to problems connected with fishing rights, which had been restricted by the Indian Act. And potlatching by no means disappeared entirely. Curtis describes a Camas potlatch held as late as 1910, at which a thousand commercial blankets worth fifty cents each and thirty goat-hair blankets valued at about ten dollars each were given away, the total amount of gifts and food representing a cost of about one thousand dollars.[10]

In the midst of these difficulties over land and rights and liquor, and even as he clung to some of his old customs, the Camas Indian embraced Catholicism with relative ease. Relations with the early missionaries—both priests and nuns—were established on a friendly basis from the beginning, with very little difficulty. It may be that in taking on the Catholic religion

---

8. Wayne Suttles, "Post-Contact Culture Change Among the Lummi Indians," *British Columbia Historical Quarterly* 18 (January-April, 1954): 94, citing *Annual Report of the Commissioner of Indian Affairs to the Secretary of the Interior* (Washington, 1895), p. 319.

9. Suttles, "Lummi Indians," p. 78.

10. Edward S. Curtis, *Salishan Tribes of the Coast*, vol. 9, *The North American Indian*. (Norwood, Mass.: The Plimpton Press, 1913), p. 72.

the Indian felt, as Suttles has suggested, that it surely must be a more powerful religion than his own, since the White man was a more powerful individual. Or possibly: "The new religion was reinterpreted to accord with native beliefs. The native may have seen Catholic worship as another means of making contact with supernatural beings in order to acquire power He may have seen Catholic tabus as parallel to those sometimes imposed by guardian spirits." [11] In "[Camas] Indian Native Culture" it is suggested that the Indian might have equated the Christian saints with the old guardian spirits, "the Thunderbird or some other bird or animal spirits, guardians of which there were many who lived in the unseen places, something like our Christian Saints, each having special powers to help us get certain things we wanted." [12]

Despite the ease with which Catholicism made its entry, and Protestantism also to a smaller degree later, in 1906 the Indian Shakers built a church on the Camas Reserve. This indigenous Indian religion—not to be confused with the Shaker community settlements of the United States—prominently features the curing of the sick, and represents a cross between Christian worship and Indian spirit dancing. Its spread in a half century from Squaxin Island in Puget Sound, where it had its beginnings in about 1881, to Vancouver Island in the north and California in the south seems to indicate that it has had something of importance to offer the Salish Indian, which he was not finding in the Catholic or Protestant churches. With the coming of Shakerism to the Camas—albeit to only a minority—we perhaps have evidence of the adoption of a new institution to meet needs and remedy frustrations accompanying the process of social change. But with this consideration, we enter the domain of the next chapters, with their emphases on the institutions of the present day, and their functions for the Indians.

11. Suttles, "Lummi Indians," p. 69.
12. Frank Morrison, ed., "[Camas] Indian Native Culture" (Paper based on panel discussion involving Morrison and three Camas Indians held at meeting of United Nations Society, Chemainus, B.C., November 19, 1952).

INTRODUCTION TO 1954

By 1954 the children of the 1870s have grown to be the old people of the band. The few of them still alive can remember when there were only one or two settlers where now the town, incorporated in 1912, thrives. Built up over five hundred acres, partly along one edge of the reserve, the town in 1954 has a population of approximately three thousand. In the center of a thriving farming and lumber region, it has attracted a diverse group of settlers, including army, navy, and civil service personnel who have built comfortable homes in the outlying districts, for retirement. It includes a small Chinatown, and a number of Sikhs, who live without segregation among the other residents. Two other White communities, much smaller than the town, but with post offices and shopping facilities, have sprung up on the edges of the reserve.

The Camas Indians, 872 in June 1954, have become merged officially into one band with the one name, Camas. This change, brought about in 1954, is purely administrative and does not affect the band council system or any of the existing living arrangements, rights, privileges. It was considered an advisable change to make because the separate bands were related groups on a common reserve, were using common trust funds, and more and more their property was being held by members who had moved out to live elsewhere on the reserve.

Each member of the band, legitimate or illegitimate, is registered in a band list, and a record is kept of his birth, marital status, death, and any transfers made in band membership. Women who marry outside of the band automatically become members of the husband's band; and anyone who transfers his membership to another band forfeits the right to own land in the band of his birth. Thus the official arrangements today tend to keep the male Indian on his own reserve, and to perpetuate patrilocal residence.

Enfranchisement—a privilege open to the Indian with the consent of Ottawa—has not occurred among the Camas, though women who have married non-Indians, or Indians belonging to bands in the United States, are no longer registered as Indians and lose the privileges of band membership. Records show that there have been thirty such cases since 1931, when data of this kind were first recorded. This does not include five women who at one time married or had children by non-Indians but are currently living on the Camas or a nearby reserve. Also, there have been five women, two men, and seven couples who were either deleted from the band list after long absence in the United States, or were known to be spending a year or more in the States. It is my impression from conversation with informants that a few more than these "stay in the States."

Since 1951 the chieftainship has been on an elective rather than hereditary basis. A chief is elected by the band to serve a two-year term, and along with him a councillor for every hundred members of the band. In 1954, eight councillors were elected from a slate of eighteen nominees. The council now meets monthly with the local superintendent (whom the Indians still refer to as the "agent") in his office and decides with him—since all moves of the band council are subject to the approval of Ottawa—boundary disputes and disposition of the band fund; that is, it makes certain allocations for housing, road repairs, food and clothing for needy members. The band fund, of which each Indian owns a per capita share, has reached, by 1954, a total of about $123,000. This has accrued largely from sale of timber, which is a band resource and can never be individually owned.

The band fund, held in trust in Ottawa, by no means takes care of the welfare needs of the Camas group, nor is it the intent of the government that it should. Numerous welfare services have been provided. Some of them are for Indians only; others are the services which are available to all Canadians. For the Indians of British Columbia, a special annual fund of $100,000 was established in 1927—in lieu of the treaty moneys which other Canadian Indians receive, and as a gesture of good will, following the years of disputes, grievances, and claims over the land question—to help provide services beneficial to the whole group as well as to individuals, furthering their efforts in agriculture, forestry, fishing. For instance, from such a fund a team of horses might be provided, or pure-bred bulls, or a power sawmill.

Additional government welfare services especially for Indians include amounts allocated for schooling, comprehensive medical services, and welfare needs such as clothing, housing, fuel, and food rations—a slightly lower relief assistance, however, than the Indians' needy White neighbors may be receiving. Other Indian privileges include reductions in train fares, special fishing permits, and special exemptions from taxation. Assistance for which the Indian is eligible as a Canadian includes the old age pension for those over seventy, the Blind Person's Allowance, Old Age Assistance on the basis of a means test for ages sixty-five to sixty-nine (with a deduction of ten dollars, however, for Indians living on reserves, because of free rent). In addition, the Indian is eligible for unemployment insurance and for the Family Allowance which provides monthly income for each child in every family from birth to the age of sixteen.

In 1948 the British Columbia Indians were accorded the right to vote in Provincial elections; and since January 1952, they have had the right to drink beer in beer parlors, though it is still illegal for them to be in possession of beer or other liquor under any other circumstances, and Indian offenses against this clause continue, in fact constituting the bulk of offenses for which the Indians of British Columbia are arrested.[13]

Along with these privileges have come some demands. The Indian Health Regulations now require the Indian to observe health legislation, and ensure that he undergoes treatment if he has an infectious disease. In 1935 schooling became compulsory between the ages of seven and sixteen, with the privilege of continuing it whenever considered advisable—though there is never an obligation to attend school after age eighteen. Furthermore, attendance is ensured by cutting off the Family Allowance if children miss many consecutive days of school.

As a result of the compulsory schooling statute, the first-grade

13. See Hawthorn, Belshaw, and Jamieson, *Social Adjustment,* p. 382.

classrooms were filled for a time with Indian children of all ages under sixteen, and it is only recently that this situation has righted itself. The young Indians of the band today—those of twenty-five and younger—are, of course, the only ones who may have had eight consecutive grades of schooling or more. The middle-aged generation may have had from one to four years at the Catholic boarding school on Kuper Island or at the Protestant school, which was located for a time at Sardis on the mainland. The grandparent generation, the Indians sixty and over, report by and large no schooling.

Two world wars have come and gone, scarcely touching the Indian. During World War II a few men volunteered, but no more than a handful were found eligible for military service. Vital statistics have relevance here. In 1944 the first and second leading causes of death among the Indians of British Columbia were tuberculosis and pneumonia, which were sixth and fifth for the rest of the population.[14]

The Indian dialect of the Camas (the Halkomelem language) is still spoken in many homes, even in cases when English is handled very well indeed in relations with the White world. The old Indian family names are no longer used in common daily intercourse, though, as we shall see, the Indians have by no means forgotten them. Early baptismal names such as "Michel" and "Pierre" have become English family names, pronounced and spelled "Misheal" and "Peall." The son of Peall is now Bob Peall; but often it has happened that the son of someone who might have been called in the early 1900s "Bob quy-o-qua-set" has become now, Johnny Bob.

We can give the reader no better image to keep in the back of his mind as he approaches the reserve in 1954 than that of the figure of eighty-six-year-old Hubert Peall, an Indian of great dignity and hardihood, eager for audience. Standing there by his hilltop home, which commands a magnificent view of the wooded hills and bay, he waves in the air, as he talks to you,

---

14. British Columbia Provincial Board of Health, *Vital Statistics of the Province of British Columbia* (Victoria: King's Printer, 1946), pp. D15–D16.

one of the printed cloth no-trespassing signs, such as are posted here and there on the reserve, and shouts: "White people aren't supposed to trespass on the reserve for fishing and hunting, but they do!" Rolling up the sign he puts it away and draws out of his pocket the copy of a letter he wrote to the governor a few years ago, a letter full of protest: "Don't let the Whites renovate the old church! If they do, that part of the land will be lost to the Indians—just as we have been losing our land acre by acre, ever since the White man came. . . ." He puts away the letter, and keeps on shouting: "The weirs have been removed! . . . Queen Victoria said the Indians would be paid for the land but they weren't! . . . All we get now is pensions! . . ."

4

Settlement Pattern and Social Organization, 1954

OVERVIEW OF THE RESERVE

A ride around the reserve today reveals recognizable clusters of dwellings at the old village sites, even though there has been considerable spreading out and building in between them, and only five of them are of any significant size. Three of the villages partly line the paved road that winds from the town down to the bay. Others are not easily seen from this trunk road or from the Trans-Canada Highway, which intersects the reserve, and are accessible only by narrow dirt roads, some of them in very poor condition, winding through the back ways. The houses of what we shall call Village I, which is at the edge of the town, stand about in the weedy fields and woods bordering the river. A few of them are built along the trunk road, in the town itself.

There are farm lands and fields of oats and hay in some of the flat areas, many of them leased out to non-Indians who do the farming; elsewhere the roads wind through the woods, over low hills, and the houses stand on very small cleared plots of ground. Gardens of any description could be counted on the fingers of one hand. There are few fences, paths, walks, or electric wires. The general impression is of a rural, nonfarming, nonprosperous type of settlement, in a region where prosperity is possible. The neat farms and homes of the White neighbors are often just across the road, or around the bend, at the edges of the Indian lands.

Here and there a few of the Big Houses built at the close of nineteenth century stand in dilapidated condition, or else topple into ruins. Their present appearance is that of old, unpainted barns. One of them is occasionally used still for winter dance gatherings, but most of the dances of this area are held in a Big House of more recent construction. Built on the old pattern, with an earthen floor, it stands in a secluded spot about three miles from town on one of the narrow, unpaved reserve roads. Families who initiate their young people as new dancers during the winter dance season can actually be found today camping in the various corners of the Big House during the winter months, fulfilling the taboos and requirements in the Indian fashion.

The one-family houses built for the Indians after the turn of the century were sometimes built across from or surrounding the Big Houses. This pattern shows up clearly in Village I. (See figure 1.) Here a number of the dwellings are grouped around a large empty area where the Big Houses used to stand.

Some of the present-day dwellings on the reserve are of recent construction; some have been standing forty or fifty years. Among the old ones are substantial two-story frame houses of Victorian design; among the new ones are both simple unpainted one-story cabins and larger houses comparing favorably with those of the White population in basic style of construction. The Indian house today is recognizable as "Indian" not because of an architectural style that sets it apart, but because of the disrepair and neglect that are so characteristic.

With all due respect for notable exceptions, in general the houses of Village I, close to the town and in the town, are kept in the best state of repair and order; whereas the houses in the "flats" village, five miles distant from the town, have declined into a general state of dilapidation that almost defies description. In the summer of 1954 all but two families there had gone berrying, and the village had an abandoned look. The houses, scattered about on both sides of the road, showed few traces of paint; windows were out, and here and there cloths were slung

OVERVIEW OF THE RESERVE

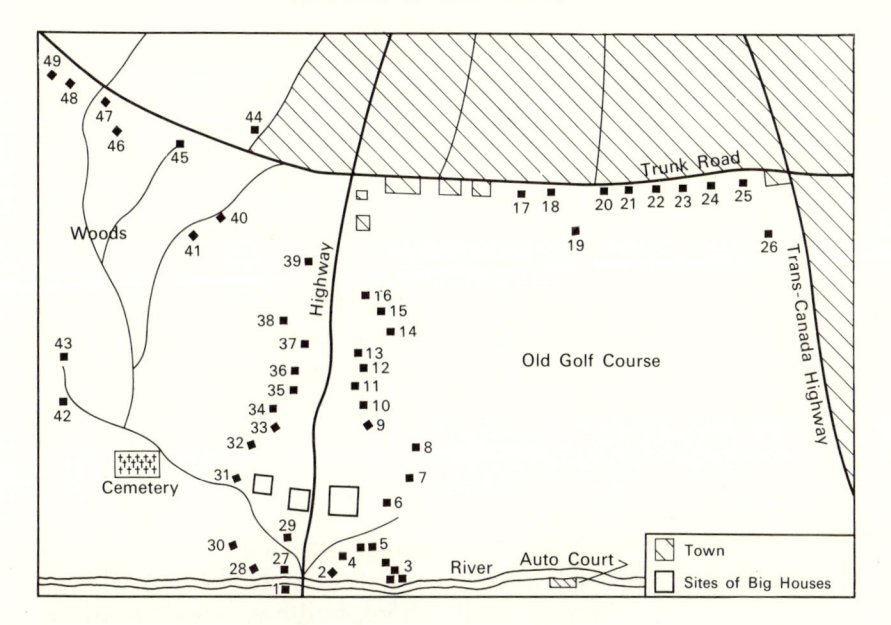

Fig. 1. Village I, showing location of houses by number.

over the open spaces, in place of glass; boards were gone from the porches. One or two new houses stood in the midst of this desolation. This is an area where water for all purposes must still be carried from the river.

Almost anywhere on the reserve—except close to the town—one may come upon an Indian home that is so draped with sacks, tires, cloths hanging on the porch, so cluttered with boxes and objects lying around beside the house, under the house, and on the porch, that the word "slum" comes to mind at once, as the appropriate word for description. It is not unusual, however, to see good cars parked out in front of such homes and electric washing machines—unused—standing in the rear.

Important as a part of the reserve scene, and providing quite a contrast, are the Catholic church, with its rectory adjoining, and the Catholic day school for Indians, bordering the reserve near Village III, in a beautiful, wooded, rolling area about halfway to the bay. These are substantial frame buildings, painted white, and kept in a good state of repair. The Catholic cemetery adjoins the church, and here many of the Indians are buried. A smaller Indian cemetery occupies a small plot of ground—tangled, unkept, and full of brambles—at the edge of Village I. The Catholic priest officiates here as well as at the larger cemetery beside the church.

The Shaker church stands by the river in Village I, a small weather-beaten, unpainted wooden structure, built in traditional Shaker style with belfry at the end opposite the entrance. Without road or walk leading directly up to its entrance, it stands in the weeds facing in a direction bearing no relation to the settlement pattern of the surrounding houses—a symbol, perhaps, of its larger than local significance. It was built to serve more than the people of Village I. Indians come to its services from as far south as Saanich at Victoria.

Also on Indian property, two or three miles from town on one of the unpaved roads, is the Protestant United Church Mission, comprising a small school building, condemned by the Indian Superintendent and closed in 1953, and a small church where occasional services are still held. These neat frame buildings, standing in a grove of ancient, giant trees, are like an oasis in the midst of the general neglect of the houses of this area.

No description of the layout of the reserve should omit description of the town itself. But this is such an important part of the lives of the Indians that it will be dealt with in a following special section.

The basic map of the land allotments made by the first local agent in the 1870s is still in use today—a valuable record, as present officials ponder over the boundaries that have become lost as streams have changed their courses in the past seventy years and as Indians have passed down their lands informally, without benefit of surveys.

Families inhabiting the old village clusters and the outlying areas near them are not restricted to the direct patrilineal descendants of the original extended families. There has been some movement in and out, as more and more sons and grandsons have come along needing plots to build on. "Aunties" and grandparents in the other villages have made land available. For instance, a group of brothers living along the trunk road inherited their land from their father, who received it through an exchange explained to me thus by one of the brothers: "Our grandfather's land was in [Village III], but there were so many sons that my late dad was left without land. So an arrangement was made by his mother, who belonged to [Village II] to have this land go to him, in payment for some debt that was owed."

In Village I alone, by June of 1954, nine families who were originally on other Camas band lists had taken up residence; while four men and one widow had moved out to other villages. Six families had come in from other bands and were not on any Camas lists, though all had close relatives in Village I. In such cases, the band council grants permission to reside on the reserve, and official transfer can be made with the approval of Ottawa. One of these families was transferred upon request in 1955. The wife, daughter of a Village I man who owns a good deal of land, wished to be in a position to inherit some of it.

However, despite circulation and some change of residence—an old custom under the bilateral kinship system—certainly each village still keeps a cluster, or clusters, of its closely related groups. Names are found in one village area that are not common in another. And reports of Indians as well as of officials in the Indian Office testify to the fact that members of the villages feel their separateness still, in spite of the common chief and council, the official amalgamation into one band, and a growing interrelatedness, which is well recognized. "We're all related," was said to me many times, by many different informants. "It's like all fourth cousins," one of them explained.

SETTLEMENT PATTERN OF VILLAGE I

A detailed consideration of Village I, which I was able to study more intensively than the other villages since I was living on its border, will amplify this picture of settlement and relationships and highlight its implications.

As previously mentioned, part of Village I is built beside the river back of the town, where formerly three or four Big Houses stood on the river bank near one of the important Indian fishing weirs at the rapids in the river. The weir was taken down by the government in 1936; the Big Houses remained standing until the early 1940s. The residents of house 4 recall when the most substantial of the Big Houses was still lived in by several families. (See figure 1.)

As the one-family dwellings were put up—some of them dating back to the early 1900s—they were built chiefly along what was then a main highway leading south from town, and some of them circled the Big Houses. Today the empty space where the old Big Houses stood looks almost like a village common, but has none of its functions. The houses around it face toward it, but it is neither park, grazing ground, nor meeting place. A remnant of the old days, it stands as a reminder of a former time, when the Indian fishing village was something completely apart from the town. Actually today the paved highway that cuts through the empty area has more significance than the area itself. Along this road—not a heavily travelled one, since the building of the Trans-Canada Highway farther out—the Indians walk or ride the quarter mile in to the stores, the beer parlors, and the superintendent's office in town.

This is not to say that their little settlement has become an integral part of the town. It retains not only its appearance of something separate, but in many respects remains apart. There are no paved sidewalks or side streets to connect it with the town. Instead, small meandering dirt roads wind uncertainly, to link the residents with the one paved arterial road. With a few exceptions, the houses stand starkly on the ground, without yards, walks, or fences. Water mains reach the area, but most houses have only a tap of cold water at the back door, and no indoor plumbing. A few houses have no water at all and are without electricity. Moreover, a number of them stand vacant throughout the summer months, sometimes from May to November, while the whole family is away berrying. During the summer of 1954 I counted four houses empty for July and August; three more for a shorter period. Many individuals spent at least a portion of the summer in the States; a few men went north for fishing.

Those houses that are built along the trunk road in town, or just off of it, appear to be more a part of the town, because of their location. About half of them are indistinguishable in appearance from the houses of the White neighbors across the street. That is, they are neat, attractively painted, and kept in good repair. It should not be supposed, however, that each one stands upon a plot of ground to which clear title of ownership has been established. The location ticket is something of a rarity these days on the Camas Reserve, due to the historical backlog of boundary confusions and the absence of surveys.

The families inhabiting the village today, though they do not trace their ancestry back to one common household, have become so interrelated that there are very few who do not have wide connections with many others, through either the father's or the mother's side. Four of the common family names are those of White men, Scotch and English, who came in with the very early settlers before the turn of the century and took Indian wives. Some of these mixed-blood families live on the trunk road in town; others are on their ancestral property in the village, next door to full-blooded Indian neighbors.

The extent of the interrelationships and their meaning in terms of everyday living can be explored by looking at the ties binding one family member to others in the village. Let us take the case of the baby born in the summer of 1954 to the young couple inhabiting house 37. (See figure 2.) This baby came into the midst of a large group of relatives on his father's side, as can be seen from consulting the legend to figure 2. His mother, who came up from Village II when she was married, has a large family of uncles and cousins there, as well as her own mother, father, brother, and sisters; however, she is not without relatives in Village I, the closest being the aunt in house 42.

The baby, however, was not the center of constant attention from all these kin; there was no frequent running back and forth of relatives from one house to another, to help, to visit, to gossip. Indeed, one Saturday afternoon at about four o'clock

SETTLEMENT PATTERN AND SOCIAL ORGANIZATION

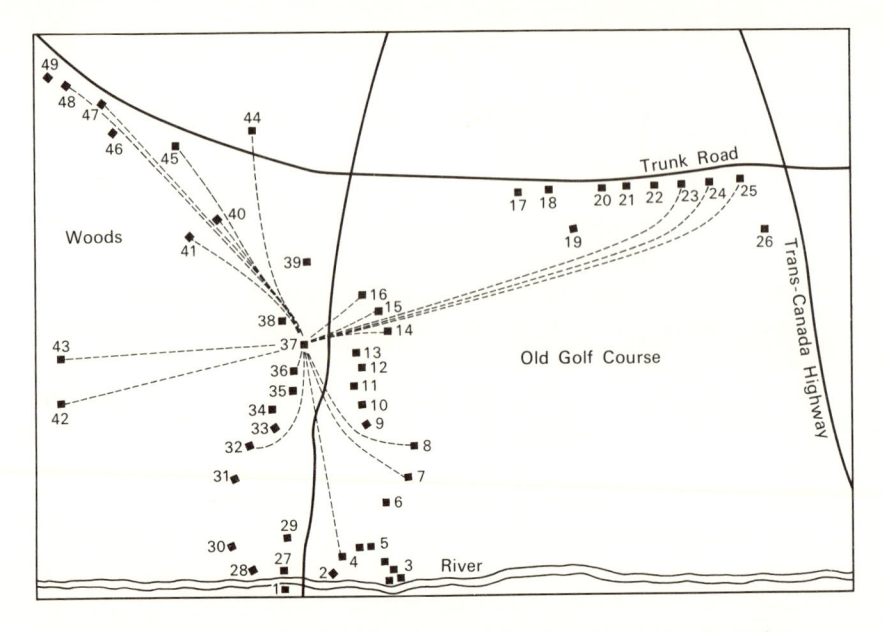

Fig. 2. Kinship in Village I. The lines join house 37 with others where there are kin. Relatives of a child in this house are listed below by house number:

 4 Grandfather's second cousin on father's side
 7 Father's uncle
 8 Grandparents on father's side, father's brother, own brother
14 Father's uncle
15 Father's uncle, grandmother's cousin on mother's side
16 Father's cousin
23 Distant relationship through great-grandmother on father's side
24 Father's cousin on mother's side, also a distant relationship through great-grandmother on father's side
25 Distant relationship through great-grandmother on father's side
32 Mother's uncle's former wife
36 Father's uncle, two of father's cousins with their many children
40 Grandfather's second cousin on father's side
41 Grandfather's second cousin on father's side
42 Mother's aunt
43 Father's cousin
44 Grandmother's aunt on mother's side
45 Grandfather's second cousin on father's side
47 Father's cousin
48 Grandmother's cousin on mother's side

I met the young mother walking back alone from town, carrying in her arms not only the new baby—a fragile premature infant, five weeks old—but two large brown paper sacks of groceries. When I offered to help carry these parcels, she accepted gratefully, saying her arm was about to break. The paternal grandparents, who might have helped out in such a situation, were away at this time, berrying.

In talking with her on another occasion, and asking her about seeing her relatives, I learned that the ones she saw most frequently were her own immediate family down in Village II, as well as her husband's parents when they were home, and that she distinctly looked down on the practice of "visiting around," as I had put it. Also, it became clear to me that in her view relatives were not always considered acceptable as friends and neighbors, merely because they were relatives. She was clearly disdainful of the large family of husband's cousins just next door, living on a considerably lower level than her own. "There's a girl there who isn't married, and has a baby every year. . . . The children break our windows."

For other families, too, the pattern was similar. Visits were made to favorite close kin—even those who lived in other bands, up and down the coast—but intimate daily contact was unusual between the remoter relatives right at hand. Many people in the village had little knowledge of what was going on even in nearby households, where they had no connections. The wife in household 30 did not know that our young mother of household 37 had brought her baby home from the hospital, even though the baby had been home for a week; the young mother in household 48 had not seen the new baby nearby in household 40. She explained that the only people in the village whom she sees are her mother, her in-laws, and her sisters. The wife in household 10, a woman in her early forties who had spent her life in that spot, could not tell me for whom the new house, number 6, had been built. The mother in household 43, which is in a solitary wooded spot, interrupted with a very definite "Oh, I *like* it," when I ventured to observe that "It's rather far off, up here."

People sat on their own porches or steps in the evening, not joining each other for neighborly chats. A real exception was the case of the aforementioned wife of household 10, who had struck up a friendship with a young mother unrelated to her, living a few doors away in household 13, and one afternoon was seen down at her house sitting in the sun on the woodpile by the door, visiting with her and her baby while her own little girl played nearby. This seemed to be a case of choice, based on standards that had nothing to do with kinship. As she explained to me later, "She keeps that baby so clean, that's what I like. And I like the way she talks. She makes sense. . . . My husband doesn't want our little girl to play with that family across the street. They aren't kept clean, and there's so many of them."

In spite of exceptions, however, the strong impression emerges that a community, or neighborhood, has not been formed, at least one in which there is daily communication and contact; and that in spite of the great network of relationships that has grown up in these years of life on the reserve, it is the *close* ties that have remained the most meaningful in daily living—those of father, mother, children, aunts, uncles, and grandparents, on both sides of the family. The residents of household 30 drove at least twice during the summer to see the married daughter living some thirty-five miles north; the eleven-year-old girl of this household goes down occasionally to one of the secluded villages near the bay because she likes to play with her cousin there; the residents of household 41 prepare to spend a holiday helping an "auntie" build a new room on her house in a locale forty-five miles north; the seventeen-year-old daughter of household 44 goes off to Seattle to visit a sister who married a Seattle man; the wife of household 10 takes a trip to Victoria to see her sister there and also one of her own twin daughters, whom this sister took to rear. Furthermore, the summer trips to the berry fields in the state of Washington are made at least partly for the fun of seeing friends and relatives, as many informants explained it. These berry-picking camps bring together Indians from a wide area and do not include White pickers.

Meanwhile, in the band council meetings, as reported to me by one of the councillors, the members have a hard time getting together. "They get to talking about their grandfathers." Another informant, not a councillor, but a prominent member of the band who attended one of the council meetings, reported: "They were out for blood. They couldn't agree. One would say so-and-so murdered his uncle or cousin. They're still thinking about it." Because of the apparent persistence of old patterns of loyalty and expectations of support from one's own headman, members of the band today find it hard to believe that the chief will accomplish anything for them, if they do not belong to his village. As one of the officials in the Indian Office put it, "The people of [Village I] come in here and say, 'We're out of it for a few years. This chief won't do anything for *us*.'"

All of these situations—the aloofness in daily living, the contacts only with close relatives, the family-oriented disagreements in the band council—suggest the persistence of the old attitudes of distrust of all except close kin; attitudes of distrust which, as explained in chapter 2, may have accompanied the belief that evil powers of other people were constantly at work to bring about accidents and mischances. It is not possible to say to precisely what extent belief in supernatural malevolence persists today, but there is some evidence that it has by no means died out completely. A newspaper article of 22 January 1956, concerning Indians in the Camas vicinity, reports: "Some Indian patients run away from N—— Indian hospital, sneak home and infect others. One runaway woman died of the disease recently in D——, convinced to the last that she was being hexed to death by enemies who had stolen some of her clothes and burned them in a churchyard."

Another bit of evidence came from one of the residents of household 36, a man in his forties, who explained his uncle's recent illness as due to a mishap brought about by ghosts. His account was something like this: "Two years ago my uncle was sitting at a table eating, and he saw the past outside—two men who beckoned to him to come out." [At this point the speaker's wife interrupted to explain to me that "seeing the past" meant seeing ghosts.] "So he went out and fell off the porch and hurt himself. He's been in the hospital two years." The Shaker practices also provide evidence of persisting belief in supernatural ways of coping with evil, as we shall see later.

However it may be, whether grounded in present fears or merely in lack of new experience to supplant the old attitudes, distrust persists. One of the Catholic priests summed it up, as he told of his difficulties in getting the Indians interested in a cooperative store. "It seems these Indians don't trust each other. They trust their own family groups, their own group of relations, but not outside of that."

There are occasions, however, when the band does unite, when the big interrelated network of kin functions cooperatively. These occasions are funerals and winter dances.

BAND UNITY

As explained to me by the chief in 1957, an "organization" exists among the Camas to ensure that everyone has a decent funeral. Individuals are asked to sign up in a book for an amount they will always contribute, for every funeral, and an appointed collector makes the rounds. "Sometimes people who have signed up for more don't give more than a quarter, but the organization is so good now that everyone can have a decent funeral." Not only must the coffin be paid for, but the gravedigger and pallbearers are also paid, as in the old days; so are others who help at the funeral. Another informant, a Village I woman who had lived there for approximately twenty-five years, explained that each locality has its gravedigger. For Village I, it is either the head of household 30 or his second cousin in household 3, both of them living here on ancestral land and tracing a common descent from a great-grandfather who occupied one of the Big Houses. "They know the things to say at the grave—the right words, or prayers, or something like that. Maybe it's not very much any more, but there used to be quite a lot of special things to say before digging a grave; they still say some of them." This informant explained also that it is still important to the Indians to have a pallbearer who is not in any way connected with the deceased. It is still felt that the father or grandfather should not touch the body or the coffin.

I did not have the opportunity to attend a large funeral (one of an important member of the band), which would have demonstrated how both the kin and non-kin cooperate on such occasions. However, even a very small funeral demonstrates it to some degree. About six weeks after his birth, the baby of our sample Village I household 37 died. He was buried in the small Indian cemetery in the village, and approximately thirty people —all but five or six of them women, mostly middle-aged or older—attended. Among these thirty were the close kin of the baby's mother and father, as well as some of the more distant kin—for instance, the grandmother's aunt of household 44 and the mother's uncle's ex-wife of 32. Non-kin were also present, including some of the residents of household 30, the gravedigger, and the man who carried the small white coffin, the head of household 12.

The Catholic priest officiated at the first part of this funeral, but after his departure the Indians continued the ceremony in their own way. The young bereaved mother broke into loud sobbing which shortly turned into a wailing chant on a sustained note, carried with a sound of "ah" and occasionally falling a note. She was joined by her mother-in-law, whose wail was even more song-like. For about fifteen minutes the two of them "sang" in this fashion—so reminiscent of the traditional way in which a new dancer finds his "song" through cries and sobs— while other women present wept softly.

When this cry-singing, or "keening," subsided, the young mother, with her own mother taking her arm, walked around distributing fifty-cent pieces to all the Indian women present. Her father then stood beside the grave, and speaking in Indian, addressed those who had helped with the gravedigging and the carrying of the coffin, called them up, and paid them larger amounts. The final act was the arranging of flowers on the grave. This was done by two of the women bystanders, after a whispered consultation with them by the mother-in-law, and a payment made to them of fifty-cent pieces. After the flowers were arranged, the assembled people began to leave the cemetery. They filed past the bereaved family, glancing sympathetically, nodding heads, shaking hands. Some just walked quietly off.

It was impossible to escape the conclusion that the funeral was not only an occasion for expression of sympathy on the part of those who attended, but also an occasion for the meaningful enacting of an old traditional rite, somewhat attenuated, to be sure, but yet a rite perpetuating the old Indian way. The father of the young mother explained to me later that the fifty-cent pieces given out are merely "souvenirs," more or less taking the place of the dishes that used to be passed out on such ceremonial occasions in earlier years. This money is supplied by the family and is not taken from the general fund collected for funeral expenses. The custom is strongly reminiscent of the old gift-giving by the bereaved family, to "dry the tears" of the recipients.

Even more significant as rites perpetuating the old ways are the winter dances, which bring the members of the band together in the winter months from January to March. The various meanings and functions of these dances to the present-day Camas Indians will be explored later. At this point it will suffice to note some of the most important features. Descendant of the old potlatching ceremonies and winter spirit dances, the present dances retain many features of the old ceremonies. Children may receive Indian names there; the swaihwe masked dancers perform on special occasions such as the showing of a photograph of a deceased kinsman; and even today a few young people are initiated as spirit dancers. Those who have previously been initiated perform at every dance, with the assembled guests participating in the singing and the beating out of the dancer's rhythms. According to Barbara Lane,[1] in 1953 there were in

1. Barbara Lane, "A Comparative and Analytic Study of Some Aspects of Northwest Coast Religion" (Ph.D. diss., University of Washington, Seattle, 1953), p. 29.

the Camas villages about fifty active spirit dancers, ranging in age from sixteen to seventy.

The large dances are intertribal affairs. The Camas group may invite the Saanich Band from Victoria or bands from Kuper Island or other points north where there are kin ties; and their own turn will come to be invited in reciprocation. Even the smaller dances bring a great many members of the band together, and this seems to be accomplished almost effortlessly. As one informant explained it, word simply "gets around" that a family is planning a dance for such and such a night.

The members of the band not only come together at these dances; they also cooperate in making them possible. Just as the old extended family group of one household used to cooperate with its headman at the potlatching ceremonies, now the large interrelated Camas "family" backs up each dance, regardless of who the original initiator of the dance may be. Though a dance is always given by an individual for a specific purpose, such as bestowing a new name or initiating a new dancer, and though the major expense falls on this individual, relatives and friends can be counted on to bring along something to give to the guests, if nothing more than a sack of apples or bag of oranges.

All informants stressed how expensive the dances are. Everyone present—perhaps two hundred or more people—must be fed, firewood must be procured and boys paid to haul it. If a new dancer is being initiated, his costume must be made, and those who guard him and help him for the four-day period of his seclusion in the Big House must be fed. Finally, gifts must be provided, including blankets, if there is a naming ceremony, and fifty-cent pieces or sugar—perhaps as much as nine hundred pounds—to "return a favor" or to "give to someone you like very much." Indeed, a family sometimes saves up for two or three years, in order to put on a dance.

It was my impression, from the remarks of the twenty individual Indians who discussed them with me, that the dances have been in the immediate past very generally attended and enjoyed "by everyone." As a White observer (a logger living in the region) described the appeal of them: "When the Indians hear those drums, they are just *pulled* to them, do you know what I mean? Did you ever experience the pull of the bagpipes? It's something that gets inside of you." Even two of the young girls who expressed fear that they might be "taken" and forced into becoming new dancers did not stay away completely on that account. "They're fun," one of them said. However, qualifying remarks—particularly about the cold—were occasionally made, indicating some falling-off in recent years, and possibly a growing disinclination to participate. As the chief himself put it: "Oh yes, everybody goes. . . . They're fading out, though. I haven't gone lately. It's too cold. They build up big high fires, and if you sit near them you're all right, but not if you have to sit a few feet away." Several pointed out that the dances are less frequent than they used to be since an effort is now made to hold them only on weekends, to satisfy both priest and Indian Superintendent. Children are no longer kept away, as in the old days, and the late hours were interfering too much with school attendance.

Only one comment indicated a direct disapproval. This was the comment of a young woman whose husband was forced into becoming a new dancer some seven or eight years ago. "His mother didn't want him to marry me. She wanted him to marry one of those C—— girls; but he didn't want to; he said she was too classy. His mother made him be a dancer; she thought this way she could get him away from me; but he came back to me. He don't dance any more. He thinks those dances are *crazy*."

As we can see, the comings and goings of the band members today follow a pattern not markedly different from that of the early days, in spite of the many changes the government has brought to pass. In the summer there is dispersal; families keep to themselves, visiting only their close kin. They see their relatives and friends at the berry fields, or else go to visit them up and down the island. In the winter the members of the band—often with their kin from neighboring bands—come together at the dances. During the fall of 1956, there were even a good many evenings of "gambling games" (also an old custom) organized by an Indian of Village I for the entertainment of the boys and young men, and held in one of the larger Village I houses.

That there have been efforts made by the Catholic church to organize band members into community activities quite unrelated to the traditional Indian ceremonies is true, and certainly they have not been unsuccessful efforts. Small beginnings, they perhaps point to possible new ways of using the Indian's potential for cooperative action. In 1954 the Mother's Club with sixteen members was meeting once a month. These women, residing in various villages of the band, were mothers of children in the Catholic day school. Organized by the priest and nuns, they now have their own president. The women make children's clothes and candy, which they sell at bazaars, using the proceeds to apply toward such needed articles at the school as a film projector, or toward a sewing machine for their own use. Also organized by the Catholic church, with the active support of the Indian Health Services nurse, is the Girl's Club, its major activity being the annual Baby Show in May of the year, when prizes for the most healthy babies are awarded, the prizes donated by a number of the stores in the town.

It should also be mentioned that the band has the use of a large hall in the armory in town (built on land rented from the band), for meetings such as elections. These general meetings, though occurring no oftener than about once a year, provide further occasions for band cooperation in a modern key. The 1953 election for chief and councillors brought out 189 of the 390 voting members of the band.

BEYOND THE RESERVE

The foregoing discussion of the settlement pattern and the band's participation in common activities within this pattern has been but a partial one. The extent to which the Indian travels, the roads he takes both within the confines of the reserve and beyond it, the locales outside of his own village that have become an important part of his life—these have yet to be made more explicit.

We have mentioned that extensive trips are taken to visit close relatives, as well as to pick berries or to follow the harvest over the border into the States. We can reiterate here that berrying may bring together people who come from such far points as Prince Rupert on the British Columbia coast, and Merritt in the interior, to say nothing of Alberni and Port Renfrew on the west coast of the island, and Vancouver.

We can also remind the reader that women have gone out to marry elsewhere; they, and the close kin of the wives who have come in to live on the Camas Reserve, are scattered up and down the island, from Comox in the north to Victoria in the south—a distance of some 140 miles. Though the majority of marriages are contracted with members of bands fairly nearby on the island, still marriages have also taken place with members of the Sechelt and Squamish Bands north of Vancouver, the Katsey Band some twenty-five miles east on the Fraser River on the mainland, as well as with the Lummi across the Strait in Washington.

Trips to see relatives, however, are not the only ones that have acquainted the Indians with life outside of the reserve. Mention has already been made of the boarding school experience that has been a part of the lives of many Camas Indians since the turn of the century. Thirteen of the twenty-six adults I queried about school experience had spent some time either in the Catholic school on Kuper Island or in the two Protestant schools, one at Alberni and the other, no longer in operation, at Sardis on the mainland. In 1954, forty-one Camas children were enrolled in the Kuper Island elementary school, and six in the Catholic high school at Kamloops in the interior of British Columbia. Other special schooling arrangements are made from time to time, which take the Camas young people some distance from their reserve. For instance, a young high school boy, failing his work at Kamloops, was sent for a nine- or ten-month course at the Vancouver Vocational Institute; a second young man was in 1954 attending the University of Washington in Seattle; and a third had had a seven-month drafting course in Ottawa and was working there.

It is questionable whether Kuper Island boarding school experience should be thought of as exposing the Indian children to the "outside world." Isolated on the island, the children live a self-contained life in their school, meeting only the White priests and nuns and other Indian children from neighboring bands. But at least there are the trips home at Christmas and in June—the ferry trip across the water and the ride on the busy island highway.

Perhaps more significant than school experience as exposure to a broader scene than the reserve itself offers is the work experience of the men of the band. The majority of those who work with any regularity do so as loggers or longshoremen. They may be up at 3:00 A.M. and off to the docks up and down the Strait, even occasionally as far north as Alberni; or they go inland to the giant sawmills on the rivers and lakes, some of them twenty or thirty miles away. This work brings them in close contact with the White man, as a fellow worker and fellow member of the union which protects the Indian from discrimination in this field of employment.

Other miscellaneous types of contact with the wider world include hospital experience in the tuberculosis hospital for Indians in the city thirty-five miles north, and for at least one Indian a hospital experience in Vancouver. A family in Village II mentioned trips to Sooke, near Victoria, to buy the wool for the sweaters knitted by the women; two mentioned vacation trips to Vancouver. And there is the important item of participation in sports, particularly by the young men of two of the mixed-blood families in Village I. These boys go down to Victoria to play with a soccer team there, or go up even as far north as Comox, a trip of about ninety miles, to play baseball with the town's Athletic League. These sports activities offer the Indian an opportunity to participate with the White man on his level, just as the logging and longshoring jobs do. In this respect, they are a contrast to what the Indian may expect to encounter always in the town on his very doorstep.

A consideration of where the Indian may go in the town, and where he does go, day in and day out, will complete our picture of the settlement pattern and bring us face to face with one of the most crucial circumstances of the Indian's life—the fact that he does not mingle with complete equality with the White man.

IN THE TOWN

Discriminatory treatment of the Indian and outright discouragement of his participation and presence were most evident in 1954 in only a few respects: One of the two beer parlors did not admit Indian women and their escorts to the ladies' section; the other admitted them but had installed a special lavatory for the Indian women, reportedly because they "made such a mess"; and the public library discouraged Indian children from taking books. "They're careless," the librarian explained. "They live on the reserve and have no telephones, and you just never know if you'll get the books back; they aren't readers; I have two or three who have cards and take care of the books all right, but I don't encourage the Indian children." The town hospital did not discriminate, but Indian patients had their own waiting room—separate from the White waiting room—at the clinic. The one movie in the town in a sense did not discriminate either, though both White and Indian informants explained that only the clean and well dressed Indians were allowed to sit downstairs among the non-Indians; the others were sent to the balcony. Finally, there was discouragement of the young Indian high school girl graduates from taking white-collar employment. Agency officials reported that it was extremely difficult for these young people to find the jobs for which their commercial course had prepared them. One applicant, a well-qualified bookkeeper, had been told frankly by one of the utility companies that she could not be hired there because she was an Indian. Employment for either educated or uneducated women was mainly as dishwashers or waitresses in restaurants.

Indian men were not employed in the town in any capacity, white-collar or otherwise, with the exception of a very few individuals such as the young man who had been trained as a mechanic and had a job in a garage and an older man who worked as a carpenter, both of them of mixed blood. This lack of employment, however, is undeniably to a large extent a matter of the Indian's lack of training and qualifications for any but the kind of job he does get, in logging and longshoring.

Certainly there is evidence that the qualified Indian is not excluded from all of the White man's cultural and civic activities in the town. Two Indians, brothers from one of the mixed-blood families, belonged to the Eagles Lodge; one of these brothers was a deacon in the Protestant United church in the town. A young man of nineteen had just been admitted—the first Indian member—to the Junior Chamber of Commerce. His talented musical uncle was a member of the town's musical club and was on occasion brought into both the public high school and the Boy Scouts to help in coaching their dramatic performances. Mention has already been made of the participation of some of the young Indian men in sports of the town.

Certain church, school, and recreational facilities were also shared by Indians and non-Indians in common. Though the Catholic and the United churches of the reserve were built especially for the Indians, there was some White attendance at both churches; and, conversely, the Indians were free to attend the Catholic and United churches in town. According to information supplied by the United deacon and a Catholic priest, some who lived near or within the town found it more convenient to attend these "White" churches, and did so.

Public schools, too, provided equality of experience. During the 1953–54 school year, there were seventeen Indian children enrolled in the town's big modern high school (including junior high), and approximately ten in the elementary schools. These were largely the children of Protestants or Shakers, as only a few Catholics prefer public schools for their children over their parochial one. In all cases of school attendance, though the parents may express choices, final decision is made by the superintendent, for it is his responsibility to select the school most suitable for the particular child and the family conditions.

All the evidence I was able to gather pointed to absence of discrimination against the Indian children enrolled in the public schools. The comments of three young people who had attended or were currently enrolled in the high school were enthusiastic. One said, "The White kids and the teachers went all-out for the Indians." A parent reported that the Indian children got elected as room representatives "just like the White kids" and had a wonderful time.

As for treatment of Indian children in the elementary schools, one mother reported: "My boy is the only Indian boy in this elementary section he's in, but they treat him real good. He's got such a nice teacher. He doesn't do very well in school—he's a daydreamer; but they're going to try to pass him from grade two. I belong to the Parent's Association. I help them out by making little sweaters; I really appreciate what they're doing for the children." Another mother, whose four children all attended a public elementary school, reported that the treatment was "not bad."

Recreational areas where the Indians participate freely with the White neighbors include the Boy Scouts, a big public hall used for such entertainment as wrestling matches and occasional social dances; and the swimming hole at the river in Village I, used mainly by children—perhaps with some tendency for Indians to congregate on one side of the bridge and White children on the other, but not rigidly so. Indians are included also in some of the town's celebrations and exhibitions. For instance, they may have a float in the Elk's parade, display handicrafts—including their famous sweaters—at the Jaycees Hobby and Home Show in the curling rink, or dance in the Dominion Day and Coronation celebrations. This dancing is only for uninitiated dancers. The real spirit dancer does not perform for the White man.

In all these latter respects, the Indian's participation is perhaps valued for its "picturesque" contribution. Certainly the Chamber of Commerce brochure on this region has featured the Indians *in costume* in the page of illustrations devoted to the Camas inhabitants, even though due respect is also paid to them as natives "whose awareness as citizens is growing noticeably."

We have pointed out that the Indian is less welcome in some

of the town's activities than in others; we have noted restrictions on some of his comings and goings; we have said that he may enter one beer parlor but not the other; that he goes freely to school, but sits in the Indian waiting room at the clinic. What we have not done is specify where he actually does go most of the time, when he goes to town. Though we have mentioned some participation with the White people in certain of the civic groups and in the churches and schools of the town, these must be thought of as fringe activities reaching only a small proportion of the Indian population. It is probably a fairly accurate assumption that the majority of the Indians who walk into town from Village I, or ride in from the remoter villages on the reserve, come, instead, for three major purposes: to go to the Indian Office, to the beer parlor, and to the cafes and stores. Many Indians patronize the grocery stores in the small Chinatown; those who are on relief or who have not been deemed responsible to handle their own Family Allowance checks pick up their needed goods at stores designated by the superintendent.

The trips to the Indian Office are for almost any purpose affecting the Indian's life, for Ottawa is still the authority and at the bottom of all essential matters of financial arrangements, housing, education, health, land ownership, and general welfare. The superintendent, as Ottawa's local representative, watches school attendance and plans the schooling of each child; he keeps abreast of the employment situation and knows which of his Indians are able-bodied and whether they are entitled to relief or not; he registers vital statistics; he sees that trust funds are set up for children of families who would drink up the Family Allowance check if left free to do so; he urges legal marriages for common-law partners; he listens to complaints.

In the fall, according to the officials, the Indians flock in, lining up fifty strong, asking for relief. They have come back broke from the berries. In the summer an old man may come in asking for some summer underwear, he has only his winter underwear, and he is too hot. A woman comes in with a little boy. He had left eighty cents in the hospital when he had been there six months ago. The hospital says it was returned here. May he have it, please? A husband and wife storm in, wasting no time with please and thank you. They are hostile over the fact that they have had to sit and wait for an hour over in the clinic. The agency explanation that this is bound to happen if they go to the clinic without appointments does little to calm them down. A man and woman come in complaining that a load of lumber has been delivered on land which is theirs. Is someone going to try to build on their land? The telephone rings. It is the department store. The man who came in with an order for underwear says he wishes to have socks also. Is he entitled to socks? Meanwhile once a month the chief and band council assemble in the Indian Office. "But only one member talks. Not even the chief has anything to say. They don't argue and think things out as they ought to," the superintendent reports.

The other well-beaten path, leading to the beer parlor virtually across the street from the Indian Office, is taken by women and men alike. Though of course there are Indians on the reserve who do not go near the beer parlors, the number of those who do is quite great enough to cause concern to the superintendent, the priest, and to many Indians themselves. The Indian Health Services nurse estimates that one-third of the women, young and old, are attending the beer parlors.

One Indian woman explained to me, "Lots of Indian women go in and sit and watch their husbands drink, but don't drink themselves; they have to be able to drive the husbands home." This was probably an account of her own experience, which she enlarged upon at another time: "Yesterday the longshoremen came in, so I knew my husband was back, and I went to look for him at the beer parlor. He was there all right, but he said he wouldn't come out; I'd have to wait for him. So I waited out there in the car from four to six, so I could drive him home—he couldn't come by himself. . . . I can't ever talk to him when he's home, he's so full of beer he never knows what I say. . . . Every time the allowance comes on the nineteenth, the men just go spend it at the beer parlor; they don't buy things for the children; some of them got no shoes, no clothes."

Another Indian woman—unmarried and a nondrinker—spoke feelingly, saying:

The woman goes off to be with her husband, and he sits on and on. She gets discouraged and starts drinking too, and the children are left alone at home with no one to look after them. A family of three children burned to death last year—left alone like that, without fire or food. They started to build a fire and then the trouble came. It has hurt the young boys too, who used to be organized in sports; but all this has gone to pieces, and they just hang around in the beer parlor.... When the beer parlor closes, they go up to the cafes in Chinatown, and this is where all the troubles start, or out on the street.

This latter fact was confirmed by the Catholic priest, who reported that Indians behave themselves very well in the beer parlors. The trouble comes later, out on the street. "The Catholic Church can't compete with the beer parlors these days," he added. "This is a bad time for church-going for the Indians. Attendance has fallen off." He mentioned also that the present attraction of the Shaker church, which "cures" Indians of their drinking habits, can be attributed to the beer parlor. "People are realizing they're going to pieces and they're looking for something to help them."

Inside the beer parlor, according to my own observation, the Indians are free to sit where they wish. They do not occupy special tables in special areas apart from the White customers. On one night of my observation, a Friday in August—a time when many Indians were still away in the States—there were fewer Indians than White men and women present; some of them were talkative and gay, others stolid and quiet—all of them, indeed, "behaving very well." No one could have singled out the Indians on the basis of their demeanor, nor indeed on the basis of their dress and grooming, except in the case of one grandmother who wore her hair tied up in a scarf.

In this chapter we have first taken a broad overview of the reserve and its settlement pattern, then drawing closer, we have considered some of the relationships and habits and ways of living that emerge from, or coexist with, this pattern. We have seen that in many respects the Camas Indian in 1954 perpetuates the ways of his great-grandfathers. He is a traveler, particularly in the summer when he goes off to see his close kin and to pick berries; but he joins with the members of his band in the winter for a season of dances and ceremonies, meaningful today as in the past.

As we pull out threads of exposition to follow along toward our conclusions, it will be particularly pertinent to remember how close the Indian of today remains to his past. Many other pieces of evidence of this closeness will emerge as we proceed. It will be important to remember, also, to what an extent the Indian is familiar with locales outside of his reserve and to what an extent he can be independent of the great web of very distantly related kinfolk surrounding him.

His independence, and his dependence, too—dependence on the superintendent as the arbiter, the "headman" who doles out relief, speaks for him in all business matters, and makes the important decisions—these will become core concepts as we develop and complete the picture of the present-day situation.

Even more basic will be the facts relative to the Indian's status among the White residents of the town—or, as we have put it, the facts relative to the places where he may and may not go. The Indians sitting in their Indian waiting room at the clinic, the high school graduates washing dishes in restaurants—these are crucial scenes in the total picture, as are the quite different scenes of young Mr. "Bob" attending the Junior Chamber of Commerce meetings; and all the Bobs sitting up there in the beer parlor with the White folks, "behaving very well" and looking attractive in their sports shirts and summer dresses.

Equally significant are the less easily observed, but no less real insignia of the Indian's differential and inferior status inherent in some of the provisions limiting his freedom, such as the restriction on free disposal of his property or free change of residence and pursuit of attractive work opportunities elsewhere; and the limitation on his access to liquor outside of beer parlors, with its resulting arrests for "offenses" from which the White man is exempt.

5

Three Households

Sketches of three households will serve as an introduction to the problems and conditions that will concern us in the family lives of the Camas. These three households have been selected as representing three different levels or patterns of striving and belief, three different modern ways of life. All have been chosen from Village I, since my opportunities for close study of households were greatest there, but it is my belief that these three represent transitional stages from old to new and that many similar households can be found all over the reserve. The first to be pictured is one where many of the old Indian ways are clung to tenaciously; in the second, the family is in some respects straddling the fence; the third is in many ways similar but represents an even more successful adoption of the White man's values, while some use is still made of the Indian traditions.

THE OLD INDIAN WAYS: PAUL HARRY FAMILY

The Paul Harry house is built on its ancestral land facing the empty area in Village I, where the Big Houses used to stand. "Right out here," said Mr. Harry, standing on his porch and pointing, "used to be the long house they all lived in in my great-grandfather's day. It extended from here out as far as the road. . . . My great-grandfather died in this Big House, and the way they took him out was they took out two boards at the end of the house, two-by-twelve boards, and because nobody was supposed to touch the corpse, two men dragged him out with a rope. . . . He's buried back here. . . . My parents lived along the trunk road, and my brothers still live there, but my mother had this property from her grandfather and wanted me to live here. I wanted to do what my mother wanted me to."

This house is not, however, the one that was built on the land thirty years ago when the Harrys settled down here to raise their family. That house burned down when the oldest son came back from the army. "He wanted some of his mother's bread so badly, he built up a great big fire. . . ." The present home is a new one, built with agency help in 1950. It is a large wooden two-story house with casement windows. It has an unfinished look, however. It is unpainted, without electricity, and stands up on foundation posts a few feet above the ground. Scattered around in the tramped-down weedy spaces around the house are old pots and pans, a child's jacket, sodden in a recent rain, and other odds and ends. The out-house stands in back among some other sheds and outbuildings. An old black car, parked at the side of the house, completes the picture. The property includes a cottonwood grove by the river and a cleared space that could be used as a garden.

The exact layout of the rooms inside the house was not ascertained, since this was one of the homes where I was never invited inside. All conversations took place on the front porch or steps.

The open front door revealed a large front room, the condition of which may have partially explained why Mrs. Harry never invited me in to sit down. It was clear to see that this family's concept of the way to furnish the living room of a house was to pattern it after the interior of the old Big House, which had nothing in it in the way of furnishings except the sleeping platform extending around the four walls, leaving space for cooking fires on the open earth floor. In Mrs. Harry's living room there were only three long, dark, and sagging couches, arranged around the walls of three sides of the room. A small wood-burning stove, for heat only, stood well out toward the center of the room. On the three couches, and under and around them, had been deposited such an amount of littered goods—shoes, papers, pop bottles, odds and ends—that it would have been difficult to find a place to sit. There were no closets or chests of drawers where such accumulated objects could have been stored, and possibly there was no concept that any such storage might have been desirable. This cluttered interior, typical of many of the houses on the reserve, appears to represent a set of values related to the old way of life. Actually, this big living room is sometimes used for local dances and gambling games in the winter, just as, in the old days, dances and games took place in the big dwellings.

Living in this household in the summer of 1954 were eleven people, making up a small "extended family." Besides Mr. and Mrs. Harry, aged respectively fifty-six and forty-eight, were the oldest son of the family, aged twenty-eight, with his wife and their ten-month-old baby; a twenty-one-year-old daughter; four younger children ranging in age from fifteen down to seven; and Mrs. Harry's old crippled mother—staying there only temporarily because Mrs. Harry's brother, who usually kept her, had gone off berrying. The oldest daughter of the family was married and living in another band.

According to the band lists, Mr. and Mrs. Harry had lived together as man and wife for nearly thirty years, and neither had had any other marriage partners. Thirteen children had been born to them, six of them dying as infants or very young children. Mr. and Mrs. Harry had been married legally, in the Catholic church, in 1933, after they had had four children. This pattern is in no way unusual anywhere on the reserve.

Mr. Harry, oldest son of a prominent Indian who was for years Indian constable, lives, as we have said, on his ancestral land. He can stand on his porch and point to some four or five other houses nearby where his second cousins live, families who trace their common descent through a group of grandmothers who were sisters. Mr. Harry and one of these second cousins are the gravediggers for the village, the men who "know the right things to say at the grave." Mrs. Harry spent her childhood and early youth in two locales—Village IV, which is one of the more secluded ones on the reserve, and Pat Bay near Victoria. She still has a sister living in Village IV and has various cousins scattered around the reserve.

Neither Mr. nor Mrs. Harry can read or write to any extent. Though Mrs. Harry says she spent two years in the Kuper Island boarding school, according to her own report she can write only her name. Mr. Harry had no schooling as a child. "I was the oldest of the children and had to help out. My mother was working for folks in the town, sometimes doing four washings a day, and my father was helping with surveying. . . . A while back the priest got me interested in going to school at seven in the evening—school for people like me; so I went and there were all those Bibles telling about how Jesus came on earth—and that's how I learned just a little reading and spelling." There was just a shade of derision in his voice as he talked about "all those Bibles"; the Harrys are not churchgoers. The four children of school age attend the Catholic day school. "Do they like it?" I queried. "Ye-e-s," Mrs. Harry drawled in a noncommittal fashion. Later developments, to be mentioned shortly, indicate some hostility to education in this family.

Economically, the Harry family is not self-supporting. Mr. Harry has not worked at longshoring, which used to be his occupation, for seven years. He describes an attack of some kind which he had while at work, seven years ago. "The doctor told me to go home and do nothing, and that's what I've been doing ever since." He occasionally brings in small sums by drying bark and selling it to a firm in town at fifteen cents a pound, to be used for medicinal purposes; also, he occasionally cuts and sells some of his cottonwood trees for pulp wood, with the permission of the band council, which gets a percentage of the sale price for the band funds. Mrs. Harry finds miscellaneous small jobs to do, such as picking up bulbs for fifty-five cents an hour at one of the bulb farms outside of town in the late summer season; also she knits and sells Camas sweaters for seventeen or eighteen dollars apiece; and according to Mr. Harry's report, he helps her with the washing and preparation of the wool. To make one sweater may take her approximately a week, if she works steadily at it.

In addition to these small bits of income, Mr. Harry draws twenty-three dollars a month relief; the old grandmother draws fifty dollars a month; and the Family Allowance money for the four young children comes to twenty-seven dollars a month in the form of goods to be collected in various stores by Mrs. Harry. This is an arrangement made by the agency to ensure that the funds will be spent for the children and not for the beer that both Mr. and Mrs. Harry find it hard to stay away from. There are neither taxes nor rent to be paid. Furthermore, the oldest son, who lives in the household with his wife and baby, is employed in logging—seasonal work, to be sure, but paying twelve to fourteen dollars a day—and draws five dollars a month Family Allowance for his own infant. The annual summer trip to the berry fields of Washington which this family usually makes probably should not be considered a source of income. The superintendent wrote in 1956 in a local newspaper article about the berrying of the summer just past: "An entire family engaged in picking [could] earn only up to eight dollars a day. Subtracted from this was the travel expenses, lodgings, board and numerous opportunities to dissipate earnings. Generally the family returned only to ask for relief." Mr. Harry, the agency says, is one of the most frequent callers at the Indian Office; he will come in practically begging for food—even though he will be seen on the same day in a store ordering a case of pop.

I found him full of complaints, rather gently voiced, about the way the government treats him. "We haven't got the electricity yet; the carpenter went away and we have to wait till he gets back.... They give us only one bag of oats and one sack of potatoes.... There's someone on the reserve who has a thousand acres and doesn't need agency help, but he's the one who gets it.... The nurse never comes around." He must have forgotten he had just told me that the doctor had been there to bring bandages for the old crippled grandmother.

He is a man who is happy to sit on his front steps on a summer morning or afternoon to talk with a visitor like myself about the old ways that survive. A dancer himself, he explains the cry songs, the spirit power concept, and says of himself: "I am the singer. I am the one who knows all the songs, and I help everybody. I'm the one who starts singing to help them at the dances. . . ." Brown and wrinkled, he speaks with a lively expressiveness of face and gesture; his English is patchy but easily understood, his voice gentle and soft, and he laughs and jokes. He is dressed in work clothes—sturdy slacks and wool shirt—that look neat and clean. He puts a gentle arm around his little girl, who comes and sits beside him for a moment.

Mrs. Harry comes out on the steps and joins us, cigarette in hand. She is a large, plump woman with a smooth and pretty face, and a friendly manner. She wears a clean flowered jersey dress, pinned at the neck with a costume jewelry "amethyst" brooch; small gold earrings hang from her pierced ears. Her English is even better than her husband's. She, too, laughs and jokes. They tell me with pride that they are teaching their children Indian now, though they are aware that people like the Gordons, a large mixed-blood family in Village I, make fun of them for doing so. "But we're Indians, why shouldn't we speak our language?"

They seem to enjoy telling me about their lively seven-year-old son and his stubbornness over learning Indian. "You should hear what he said to me yesterday," Mr. Harry laughs. "He said, 'I don't *want* to, and you look like a Chinaman when you talk to me like this!' "

The four young children spend most of their time on these summer days swimming in the river, just a stone's throw away, coming home to eat only when they are hungry. If it is a day when the "old woman," as Mr. Harry laughingly calls his wife, is off picking up bulbs, then the eight-year-old girl may have charge of her baby nephew, while her oldest sister and sister-in-law take care of the cooking and washing.

This little eight-year-old, unlike her parents (but like many of the small children of the reserve) has a neglected and unclean appearance. Her mop of shaggy hair hangs down on her face like a gypsy's; she wears a loose skirt that is much too large for her; tiny gold earrings adorn her pierced ears. The baby, whom she may push in his stroller up and down the road, looks like an almost completely neglected waif, for he is a little past the baby-in-arms stage, which is the only period when many Indian parents manage to keep their young children clean. Now there are scabby sores on his head; his nose drips and his face needs a good wiping; his clothes are dirty and his diapers wet. But he appears happy in the care of this tender, motherly, and highly competent little eight-year-old. She pushes the stroller onto the bridge, stops halfway across, and turns the stroller so that the baby can look down to the river below. "See the boys swimming, baby?" she says, in a motherly tone. In a moment she is supervising one of the swimming children, a girl of about eight or nine, as well as the baby in her care. "You're in the deep water!" she calls down loudly, in admonition.

On another day, when she claims she has the baby in her charge for the entire day, she accompanies us all the way down the road to our auto court, pushing the stroller along, with its occupant in his usual wet, grimy condition. We give her some milk and cookies, which she immediately shares with the baby, and then we ask her to go home, explaining that it must be her lunch time, and anyway we have work to do. But she refuses to go, saying that she doesn't need to go home for lunch until she is hungry. She wants to stay, and there is simply no budging this strong-minded, independent little creature until she is ready to go.

She and her seven-year-old brother have great freedom to roam around and play, unsupervised, in the summertime when there is no school. Even when she is saddled with the care of her nephew, she says she likes it, that she'd rather care for the baby than do anything else. "I know how to fix his bottle. . . . I know how to change his diapers when he's wet." She has time, however, to play with her various cousins and other nearby children in the neighborhood and to go in to town by herself if she wants to. She was seen doing so on one occasion, with seven cents her big brother had given her to spend for candy.

She seems to be at home in a world of friendly adults. On this walk into town, she sees a young man in his twenties across the road—her cousin, she says—and she calls out "hello" to him in an easy, natural way. On another occasion when we have gone to talk with Mr. Harry's second cousin, Jack Harry (the other gravedigger in the village, living across the road) she and her younger brother are there playing with the cousin of that household. As we stand in the doorway talking with Jack Harry, a large soft-spoken man with a rather mournful air, the two children scuttle in and out between us, or stand beside the gentle man for a moment perfectly at home.

Jack and Paul Harry are both strong supporters of the old ways. On one occasion I talked with them together at Paul Harry's house. They brought out their rattle sticks (for use at winter dances) to show me, and also some comic masks and a drum with design painted by Mr. Jack Harry. They agreed that "the old ways are dying out. There are only a few people like us who are keeping them up." Both are initiated dancers. Mr. Jack, in addition, is a Shaker. This means that he can dance and sing, in the old Indian way, all during the summer as well as winter, for the Shaker services combine Indian dancing with some of the Christian forms of worship.

By 1957 there have been developments in the Paul Harry household that illustrate further how the Harrys are living close to the old ways.

A new home, a low modern house which is something of an anomaly standing there in the weeds of Village I, has been built for the oldest son, with help from the agency and the band fund, on his father's property close to the Paul Harry house. There are three little children in this family now, who spend most of their time during the day at the Paul Harry house, since both their father and mother are working.

In the Paul Harry household itself, an "extended family" is still in residence. Mrs. Harry's old invalid mother now lives there permanently. Newcomers are a common-law husband of the eighteen-year-old daughter, and his nephew, a boy of about eleven who has no one to look after him during the summer vacation period when he is not in the Kuper Island school. "His mother drinks," Mrs. Harry explained, and she also made it clear that this child was in her son-in-law's care, and not her own. "My son-in-law looks after his nephew." Also new in the household is a young child of about three, illegitimate son of the twenty-four-year-old daughter, who now lives in another band with a man who is not the father of the child. The Harrys have raised the grandson as their own child from the time of his birth. Thus the house is a refuge for various kin who need help, and the grandparents are prominent as caretakers for the young children. The little grandson, it should be added, is treated tenderly and mothered by all the females in the house. His grandfather, too, is a tender caretaker. On one occasion when I was sitting talking with Mr. Harry on his front steps, this little boy came and sat between us for a while. He was sucking a lollypop, and once held it up to his grandfather's lips, to share it with him. When he reached out and touched my bracelet, Mr. Harry drew him gently away, in a quiet and casual manner, hugging him to his side.

I inquired why the eighteen-year-old daughter had not gone to her husband's home to live and was told that one of his folks was in the hospital and the other only a step-parent. No doubt one of the reasons why the groom was welcomed in the Harry home was that he was working and could contribute groceries.

Actually, during the summer of 1957 this young couple moved out and decided to try living with the groom's step-parent, a shift brought on by a series of conflicts between mother and daughter, symbolic of some of the conflicts between the new and the old ways. The Harrys, according to the agency's belief, had been trying in every way they could to keep this daughter close to the old Indian ways, though she was only half through a year at the Kamloops boarding school, where the agency would have made it possible for her to stay. Also, the family initiated her as a new dancer during the winter of 1957. And now, for ten months, they had been sanctioning the common-law marriage and refusing to give permission for a legal ceremony. The girl herself was eager to make the marriage legal. She came to the Indian Office in tears one day during the summer of 1957, announcing that she and her husband were moving out of the Harry household. "My mother just fights with me all the time and drinks and says dirty things and won't sign to let me get married." This young girl was as attractively dressed and groomed as any young Canadian high school girl might be, and she wore a wedding ring.

That her family, though on relief, could find a way to stage the expensive dance initiation well signalizes the importance to them of keeping up the old ways. It was a small ceremony, as winter dance ceremonies go, and was held in their own house rather than in the usual Big House down near Village II. The girl was kept there in seclusion for four days and nights while she "found her song," and during that time a "nurse" watched over her. Food was provided by the Harrys; and when the guests came for the dance ceremony itself, they were not only given a big meal, but, as Mr. Harry explained, "I get maybe fifty pounds of sugar and give each one maybe two pounds." Relatives who were as eager as the Harrys to keep up the old customs helped with the expenses. One of these was the cousin, Jack Harry.

Mr. Paul Harry was still not working, though a recent physical examination had shown him to be in good health. The agency was a little uncertain as to how it was going to deal with Mr. Harry and his conviction that he was an invalid.

BETWEEN THE OLD AND THE NEW: BILL GORDON HOUSEHOLD

In the next household that we shall examine, there is also a large extended family; Indian is the language spoken at home; there are problems of drinking, and marital conflicts; here in this family, too, at least one of the young people has been initiated as a new dancer; but on the other hand, there are some determined efforts to cope with the drinking, to send the children to school and church, to keep a neat and clean house, and to hold a firm hand over the wild ways of the adolescent girl.

Bill Gordon, a strong, heavy-set man of sixty-seven, is commonly called "Chief Gordon." He was one of the village chiefs before the elective system, and traces his ancestry back to a very early chief whose daughter took a White man for a husband. He himself shows very little trace of Indian blood.

He and his four younger brothers, who are settled there in the village near him, own large tracts of village land. Bill Gordon rents out some of his land along the trunk road to the town's Agricultural Society. It is because of his steady income from this land that the agency does not accept children from the Gordon household for the Kuper Island boarding school. "Chief Gordon has lunch for them," they say.

Mr. Gordon works intermittently, as do many Camas men. During the summer of 1954, according to his daughter's statement, he was spending most of his time in the beer parlor; but in the summer of 1957 he was working at longshoring.

Bill Gordon and his wife, a woman of his own age who is more Indian in skin color and features than he is, have raised seven daughters, some of whom are still living, for various reasons, with their families close to the paternal nest. "I have forty grandchildren and twelve great-grandchildren," Mr. Gordon says with pride. Band lists do not indicate that either Mr. or Mrs. Gordon had any previous marital partners. The marriage was registered as "legal" as long ago as 1931, when the census was first taken.

The house the family occupies is one of the oldest in the village, built at the turn of the century by Mr. Gordon's father. In its heyday it must have been a rather fine house, standing there by the main highway. It is a one-story frame structure of sturdy construction, with a long front porch, bay windows, and "gingerbread" decorations. It still carries traces of a coat of paint. It did not have electricity, however, until 1957, and the water supply is only a single tap of cold water at the back door. The two front rooms have separate entrances off the front porch, providing some privacy for the two main nuclear family groups within the large extended family living in this house.

Mr. and Mrs. Gordon live on one side of the house, and with them is their thirty-one-year-old daughter Phyllis and her seven illegitimate children—the first five of them by one man who acknowledged the paternity, but who was not married to the girl and finally deserted her; the sixth by a Mexican; the seventh by an Indian who finally married her in 1956. Also with Mr. and Mrs Gordon, off and on, is a twenty-year-old granddaughter, child of one of their daughters. They took the child in when the daughter, left a widow, went off to live with a second husband in another band.

The other side of the house is occupied by the thirty-five-year-old married daughter, Margaret, her husband, and seven of their eight children, ranging in age from seventeen down to an infant of a few months. "I never did go up to my husband's band when I married him. He didn't have any land or house there. His folks were dead." Margaret has not always lived here in her father's house, however. Her residence has been a shifting thing. At one time, fearing that the old house was making her children sick, she and her husband tried life in Seattle for a while. They have also lived for a time in a house just next door. The Gordon household appears to be over-run with children. Fortunately, there is play space in the weedy empty area of the village, not far from the Gordon house. When a group of Gordons, cousins, and neighbors is playing out there, it looks like recess time for a whole school.

Directly across the road from the Gordon house lives another daughter, who has been occupying "temporarily" for about two years a mere shack with her husband and their son John and his wife and baby. This daughter has returned to live here so that she may inherit some of her father's land. Her husband is in the process of getting a transfer into the Camas Band. Their boy John spent a part of his childhood in the Gordon household with his grand-parents; his return is like a return home. In the summer of 1957 when his wife had a new baby, he and she stayed for a while with Chief Gordon.

Other details could be added concerning the shifting picture, the comings and goings of the kin who use this household. But in order not to end in confusion rather than clarity, suffice it to say that Chief Gordon's function among his kin appears to be something like that of the early heads of households: aid is extended to the needy; the house is home for a large group of relatives.

However, when he ran for chief in the recent elections, along with one of his younger brothers, the kin group supported the younger brother and not the old chief. Could this be partly because old Chief Bill and his wife have become regular habitués of the beer parlor? According to the agency, Mrs. Gordon is one of the "worst drinkers" on the reserve.

The interior of Chief Gordon's side of the house, the only time I saw it, in 1957, seemed to reflect an almost complete lack of household care. Living in it at the time were Mr. and Mrs. Gordon, nine children of daughter Phyllis (who with her husband had gone off berrying), and grandson John and wife and new baby. I was taken in by daughter Margaret to see the new baby and found myself in the midst of such a horde of children milling around among beds so rumpled and strewn with clothes that it was hard to concentrate on the baby. I did take in the fact that in the midst of this disorder, two boys of about eleven or twelve, sitting on the humps of clothes on one of the beds, were forking chow mein out of a carton, something obviously bought in one of the Chinatown stores. I know of no better way to describe the room than to say it was an absolute shambles. Mrs. Gordon, wearing a bandanna tied on her head, as many old Indian women do, stayed mainly in the back part of the house while I was there. She speaks only Indian.

On Margaret's side of the house, however, it is an entirely different story. Though three saggy-looking double beds crowd the front room, they are neatly made up. One corner of the room is curtained off as a closet. There is also a chest of drawers to hold clothing, and there are no odds and ends lying about. On a table, clean dishes are neatly stacked.

Margaret, a pretty woman with a ready laugh, keeps herself attractive. She has a home permanent wave and wears flowered print dresses and little dangling pearl earrings. Proudly she tells me that she got legally married when she married, and that now all her sisters but one have had the legal ceremony. "My oldest sister couldn't, because she was Roman Catholic and the man Methodist. She's the one who lives in Seattle. She married a White man."

Margaret had only one year of schooling herself, but wanted

to go very badly as a child and cannot understand children who do not like school. "I had to stay home and baby-sit for my youngest sister, but I wanted to go so bad that sometimes I'd run off and take the baby along, and put her down on the floor there." Margaret's own children are going through the Catholic day school. She would like to have the oldest daughter, Elsie, go on to high school, and as a matter of fact, all the arrangements were made for her at Kamloops but Elsie refused, and ran off to the States. At home now, turned seventeen, she is a problem to her mother, who is kept busy trying to keep her from "going crazy," as Margaret calls it. We were informed at the Indian Office that the girl was to be brought into court for going into beer parlors.

Another of Margaret's worries was that Elsie was a member of a girl gang that hung out with a teen-age boy gang, the Black Hawks, a group causing concern to a number of Indians. A band council member who discussed the Black Hawks with me explained, "They're not so bad as they were. I got ahold of the ones who were organizing it and told them they'd better toe the line or I'd see that they landed in jail." He believed that the gang was mainly composed of some of the uneducated "flats" boys against the Village I boys and particularly one Gordon boy—a nephew of Bill Gordon—attending the public high school. He did not know of a girl gang. Margaret's version—possibly exaggerating the numbers involved—went something like this:

> There are about seventy of these teen-age boys in this gang, from around here and the flats. They're copying the funnies. They have whistles and hide around, and when that whistle blows, they all come out of the bushes. One night I heard a whole bunch of them was up at the Shaker Church, just waiting around outside for people to come out. They were going to get 'em. I went up there and there they were, just sitting around out there, a whole crowd of them; they all wear these jackets, just alike. . . . I had to go out in my kimono with my coat over it. My Elsie had been gone for hours. She said she was going out to the toilet, and she went out the back door, but didn't come back. I found her up there and brought her home.

The girls have their gang, just like the boys, and join up with them. They like to fight, too. One night my Elsie came in here with a big gang of girls, and they put the screen up and went behind it and changed into their jeans and jackets. I notice Elsie's got a different color one from the rest; hers is sort of wine-colored, and one other girl's is, but the rest are that navy checkered kind. Maybe Elsie's one of the leaders, I don't know. They wouldn't tell me.

One night recently Mrs. C—— saw them and thought two of the girls was gettin' into a fight, and she called the cops and they came and put the girls in jail [laughter] but let them go; said they'd give them another chance.

These Black Hawks wait outside the beer parlors on Friday and Saturday night, to beat up the ones they've got it in for. They hang around in Chinatown, too. That's where they get the liquor.

They're against the Gordons and the Scotts. They don't like people who are half-breeds, half White.

Elsie, in the summer of 1954, was a young teen-ager whose bright, clean face was marred only by a set of bad teeth—commonly the case among the Camas. She dressed in neat blue jeans, and took pains to fix her hair prettily. Lively, chatty, friendly, she talked easily with us. By the summer of 1957 her troubles were over. She was safely married, living in another band, and expecting a baby. "No more Elsie," her mother said, a little ruefully.

Margaret's troubles with her husband, Ed, were continuous, however. A handsome young Indian, dressing very snappily in tropical sports shirts, he was a drinker, and also—according to Margaret in 1954—was staying with another woman on weekends. Margaret was determined to keep him with her and to try to make him take care of his family. "I don't want these kids to be kicked around. If Ed left me it would be hard on them. Stepfathers don't like the children so well. . . . I'm not going to let him get away from me until I die!" She claimed that when she knows he's gone off to this other woman, she goes to the sheriff and gets a summons. This scares him, and he comes back.

She was one of the women who, finding that her husband had come in from his job and had gone off to the beer parlor, would go and try to get him to come home. Failing this, she might sit and wait for him in the car in front of the beer parlor for as long as two hours, so that she could drive him safely home. She also occasionally went with him to the beer parlor in the evening, abstaining from beer herself, so I gathered, but sitting there with him. Apparently she was attempting not only to hold her husband in this way, but to exercise some control over him. On these evenings when she went to the beer parlor, she paid a neighbor woman to baby-sit for her children.

She was trying to give her children what she considered a good break. They went regularly to school; she had found the thirty-five dollars necessary for the thirteen-year-old's school graduation dress; she took the children to church quite frequently, so she said; and she had managed to get some of her little boys active in the Scouts in town. Yet for all this, Margaret had some of the values and ways of the Indian that are at variance with those of the White man. She did not succeed in keeping her small children clean. The new infant, to be sure, was spotless, but the nineteen-month-old boy, scuttling around on the floor, was damp all over and covered with dirt, his runny nose unattended to. Moreover, Margaret had the attitude toward children that enabled her to leave some of them with relatives for months at a time. Loving to go off to the berry fields in the summer, she once left one of her young ones behind with a relative for three months, so that she could go, and the nineteen-month-old child was left for a time in Seattle with the sister there, simply because this sister liked having a child around and had none of her own.

Margaret, too, had become a strong believer in the Indian spirit power concept, though she herself was not an initiated dancer. She had seen what had happened to her nineteen-year-old son, who two years ago became a dancer. "I didn't used to believe in these dances, but now I do, since I've seen what they do to my son. People get sick when they are dancers. He'd just lie here—I wouldn't have believed it if I hadn't seen it with my own eyes. He can work in the summer, but in the winter he's sick. His wife is a dancer, too. They're both down in the States now, doing farm work." She was serious and earnest not only about the winter dances, but about her husband's stumbling attempt to tell me how his uncle had seen ghosts who caused him to have an accident and hurt himself.

She gave the impression of being a strong individual, and capable of strong pride and stubbornness in her dealings with the White man. Particularly illustrative of this was her account of how she reacted when the agency made preparations to install electricity in 1957.

> That man from the agency came and looked all around my room, said they were getting ready to put in lights, but why was I here, and did I expect lights? I belonged to W—— B—— Band, didn't I know that? "Well, sure I belong to W—— B—— Band, but my husband never lived there, that's why we're here," I said. "His father died when he was two and he was raised at F——. He hasn't got any place at W—— B——. We've always lived here. Is there somebody doesn't want us here? What harm do I do? Do I ask for food from anybody? And did I ask for lights? I didn't. Why do you come here to put them up?"
>
> Well, he went away, and after a day or two the men came in to put in the lights. "What are you doing here?" I said. "I don't get any lights. The agency says I don't belong here, I belong to W—— B—— Band."
>
> They said if they were going to put them up in the next room for my dad they'd have to put them here. But I said, "No you don't. I don't want any lights. What are you doing here?"

Margaret seemed to enjoy reliving this battle of the lights, as she recounted the episode to me. Her protest was evidently the part of it that appealed to her the most, for she did not even go into the details that would explain how it was that in the end the lights were installed.

Her children have some of this same quality of strength. Whenever I visited the home, the children ran up to stare at me very openly. There was never any shrinking away. Even the youngest ones were forthright in their remarks and questions. On my last visit, I found the three-year-old girl and five-year-old boy sitting in the front seat of the car, parked in front of the house. They were pretending to drive. "Where's your car?" they called out to me inquisitively, noting that I was walking this time, instead of driving. This query was immediately followed by a very adult remark on the part of the three-year-old, who anticipated my purpose in coming. "My mother's home," she announced.

I stood chatting on the porch for a while with both Margaret and Ed. Suddenly in the midst of the conversation, Ed broke off, and looking toward his pert little girl there in the front seat of the car, said with the tone of affection not at all unusual among Camas parents, "That's my baby sitting there."

Probably neither the Indians nor the White residents of the town would say that the Gordon family is prospering. The elder Gordons have slumped into drinking and have not kept up their house. The daughter Margaret is struggling against odds to maintain standards.

NEW WAYS: FRED WILSON FAMILY

In the next household that we shall turn to—that of the Wilsons—prosperity and high standards in the White man's terms are very evident. That this condition may not be an unmixed blessing for the Indian living on the reserve today will suggest itself, as we look at the way of life and attitudes of this family as well as the attitudes of others toward the family.

The Wilson house itself, newly built in 1949, looks a little out of place standing on the barren ground of Village I, not far from the river. It is a house that might better belong on one of the nicer streets of the town. Planned and built by Mr. Wilson, it is a large two-story frame house, neatly painted, with venetian blinds at the windows. It has electric lights, telephone, and indoor plumbing. The furnishings in the immaculate interior include over-stuffed velour davenports and arm chairs, a "walnut" bedroom suite, a chrome-trimmed dinette set, a large radio-phonograph, and four shelves of magazines and paperbound books. The only indication that this is an Indian interior is the arrangement of the furniture in the living room. It all hugs the walls, as in the Harry house, leaving the central floor space empty.

The Wilson family has never lived in extended family style. Only Mr. and Mrs. Wilson and their unmarried children are the occupants of this house. Mr. Wilson, aged sixty-two, is the grandson of a White man and a native woman from the flats. Still owning some land down in the flats, he came up to Village I at least twenty years ago to settle on a parcel of land he inherited from an aunt.

Mr. Wilson "parted" from his first wife some time in the 1920s, when she went off to the States taking her two daughters with her. Her name was finally deleted from the band list, but since Mr. Wilson was legally married to her, he was not free to enter into another legal union. His second wife, the present Mrs. Wilson, was taken in the Indian common-law way, without benefit of legal ceremony. Six children were reared, and a marriage ceremony was only very recently performed, upon news of the death of the first wife. The present Mrs. Wilson, aged forty-nine, had been previously married to a White man who left her a widow with one daughter. This daughter is now married to a prominent and able Indian of Village I, and one of their children is indistinguishable in appearance from a White child. Mrs. Wilson herself may have some White blood. Though she comes from a band a little farther north, she says that her father and Bill Gordon's father were cousins. However, in spite of the strains of White blood on both sides, neither Mr. nor Mrs. Wilson looks entirely White, nor do any of their children. The four girls and two boys, ranging in age from twenty-four to eight, are a fine looking, well-dressed, well-groomed group. The two oldest girls have married into the Gordon and Scott families, and are rearing handsome children.

High school graduation has been and is the aim of Mr. and Mrs. Wilson for all their children. The oldest girl stopped school after ten grades to get married, but by 1957 the three other daughters had graduated from the public high school in the town, and the other younger children were progressing steadily through school—the youngest one in the Catholic day school. According to Mrs. Wilson, it was hard to manage financially when the three daughters were in high school at the same time, but an arrangement made for buying on credit from some of the stores in town was a great help.

Jobs have been difficult for these educated girls to find.

Though well trained for secretarial work, they are among those we have already mentioned who have been turned down flatly simply because they are Indian. The agency has employed two of them, from time to time, and one has been a cashier in both a restaurant and a grocery. In the summers they—but not Mrs. Wilson—go to the States to work in the berries or in a cannery where their mother feels they are well treated and safe, since the "boss" of the employees is an Indian woman from Village I, well known to the family.

Chaperonage has been careful in this family, and none of the girls has gone through such "wild" periods as young Elsie Gordon was going through in 1954. One of the married daughters, who married at about twenty, says that she never went with any other boy than the one she married; in fact, her mother refused to allow her and her sisters to go out at all except to movies. As children, they were not even allowed to attend the winter dances, and none of the family is an initiated dancer.

Mrs. Wilson speaks deprecatingly of the way many parents have let down standards these days. "My own parents wouldn't think of letting children be present if rough talk was going on, the way many parents do today." She herself lives an industrious domestic life, scarcely ever stirring from her home except to go with the family to the Catholic church on Sunday and to occasional winter dances, and in speaking of the dances she made it clear that in her opinion these dances were for amusement only. "They are not a religion. We're Catholics." She busies herself with the housework and with the making of sweaters, washing and preparing the wool in the summer, and knitting in winter. Her sweaters are sold in a sporting goods store in Vancouver. Needless to say, she has never gone near any of the beer parlors. She feels it disgraceful for women to go into them and believes that it is access to the beer parlor that has "ruined" the Indian. Though her husband does not stay away from beer completely, he is not one of the heavy drinkers on the reserve.

Mr. Wilson's prosperity has come from several sources. He has worked at logging and longshoring, has operated a hay bailer, has been "boss" of a hop yard, organizing its crew of pickers; he has also been a buyer for a logging outfit. With his educated children and his modern, well-furnished home, he stands out as an Indian who has been making good in the White man's terms. Interestingly enough, he seems also to be trying to make good in at least some of the Indian terms, as well. Though he has never let any of his own children become initiated dancers, he has been one of the leaders on the reserve in organizing winter dances for the band, and in promoting them through generous contributions of goods as well as of his time and organizational ability. It was he who recently staged a traditional "naming ceremony" for one son and daughter, at a cost of around fifteen hundred dollars. It was he who in the winter of 1957 organized some of the traditional Indian gambling games, held in Paul Harry's home, for the entertainment of the young people of the reserve.

A White informant connected with the agency suggested that Mr. Wilson's activity in promoting the old Indian ceremonies might be related to a desire for prestige, since in the 1954 elections he was running for chief. It was also the opinion of the same informant that Mr. Wilson's prestige among the Indians was not high; that, indeed, he was perhaps both feared and disliked. The story was told of how the Indians invite him into the beer parlor and attempt to humiliate and "worry" him by manipulating him into having to pay for a whole tableful of beer.

If his prestige is not high—and the fact that he received only 32 of the 189 votes cast for chief may bear this out—there are probably several reasons for it. One opinion, voiced by the same informant, was that in Mr. Wilson's timber deals for the logging outfit, the Indians come out the losers. I have no way of corroborating this. Even without such an explanation, there is another very plausible one, expressed by one of the Catholic priests in discussing another family in very similar circumstances: "The Indians don't accept this family. They're halfbreeds, and the Indians don't like White people to mingle with them. And the White people are quicker. It's hard on the Indian's inferiority complex."

The priest may be mistaken in his assumption that the White people are necessarily "quicker." The way of life of the Wilsons and other similar families may represent the *desire* to move toward the White man's ways and values, augmented by a greater ease in doing so because of White connections. And it may be this desire and its consummation that offend some of the more tradition-bound Indian families.

It looks, however, as though the Wilsons are by no means turning their backs on their Indian membership and heritage. They are in the difficult position of trying to remain Indian though adopting many of the White values. It seems a plausible hypothesis that at least a part of the motivation for Mr. Wilson's sponsoring of costly Indian ceremonies may be to relieve a sense of conflict in values and way of life. His accumulation of expensive goods for the comfort of himself and his immediate family is in line with the White man's code of a good life, but is in direct opposition to the Indian concept of status through ability to give lavishly. The Indian never accumulated goods to embellish his own life, to set himself apart from others. The majority today—even the chief of the band—still live in homes approximating the conditions of crude temporary camps.

A brief look into the household of one of the married daughters of this family will complete the picture and provide a contrast to situations of some of the other young people already mentioned—the Harry's eighteen-year-old daughter, for instance, illegally "married" and in conflict with her mother over the marriage; or Margaret's nineteen-year-old married son, lying around "sick" on the couch during the winter, unable to work because of the spirit power welling up in him.

Vera Wilson, now aged twenty-two, married Henry Gordon, twenty-three, son of one of Bill Gordon's brothers. This brother, Peter Gordon, who has served as one of the elected chiefs of the band, has an industrious wife who keeps an immaculate, though outwardly unpretentious, house.

My records do not indicate whether Henry finished high school before the agency made it possible for him to take a mechanic's course in a vocational school. It is likely that he had at least some high school education. His parents are sending a large family of children through the school, just as the Wilsons are. Henry has a younger brother who married a young White elementary school teacher in 1956, and settled down in the town with her.

With their two babies, eighteen months and four months, Henry and Vera live in a new bungalow-style house built by Peter Gordon, with some agency help, on a piece of Peter Gordon's land only a short walk from the Wilsons. In 1954, when I saw the interior of the house, it was still so new that the young couple had not had a chance to finish it off or completely furnish it, and the yard was a mass of weeds. The living room was almost empty, but the kitchen had been more or less finished, and it was a spacious, bright, clean room. Though the only running water was a tap at the back door, there was a modern sink, and other conveniences included an oil-burning stove and a breakfast table and chair set. The house had electricity and there was a radio in the kitchen. White flour-sack curtains had been made pretty with inserts of yellow bands. There were various little decorative articles around, such as ornate salt and pepper shakers and a little cedar chest.

Vera was a member of the Girl's Club of the Catholic church and had won prizes at its baby shows for her healthy, beautiful babies. Unlike the babies of approximately the same age in the Harry and Gordon households, her eighteen-month-old boy had no sign of a sore or a scab on his skin and was kept relatively clean and dry, even though he had reached the exploratory stage and was into everything. Vera took him regularly for check-ups to the Indian Health Services nurse, and was trying to follow the nurse's suggestions for care and feeding.

Busy with her children and her housekeeping, Vera expressed very little interest in the winter dances. "I've been sometimes," she said, but corrected me when I remarked, "I hear that everybody goes." "No, *not* everybody goes," she said. Her husband holds a regular job as mechanic in a garage in town and belongs to the mechanics' union. He has further close contacts with White men as an outfielder on the town's baseball team. This young pair appear to be trying to head for a new way of life that includes very little of the old. There are others like them.

The foregoing sketches have been offered as springboards for discussion of present-day Camas values, as they are embodied in the household life and the roles of family members, and in such manifestations as drinking, Shakerism, and participation in winter ceremonies.

Additional questions of importance may seem to have been posed, namely: What is the role of the Indian of mixed blood in the changing picture of Indian society? Is he one lap ahead of the others in the desire or ability to fit into the White man's pattern? Is he, as Barnett found in one study, among those who are preeminently the acceptors of cultural change?[1]

It was not with intent to suggest this conclusion that the Wilsons were chosen in this study to represent a family moving toward the White man's way. It is my belief that a few such families could be found among the ostensibly full-blooded Indians on the reserve, in both the older and younger generations. However, data are lacking which would make it possible to explore here any hypotheses relative to this question. The band lists do not contain information about White ancestry in Indian families. It is my belief that there may have been a good deal of White infiltration, to say nothing of Mexican, Filipino, and Chinese, and this is corroborated by Hawthorn, Belshaw, and Jamieson, writing of the Indians of British Columbia in general:

> The population officially classed as Indian is by no means fully Indian in racial origin. A great deal of admixture with Whites had occurred before the registration of Indians began, and with realism the Department did not open inquiries into the racial origin of individuals, but classed them on the basis of social facts, principally on admitted membership in a band of Indians.[2]

1. Homer G. Barnett, "Personal Conflicts and Cultural Change," *Social Forces* 20 (December, 1941): 164–76.
2. H. B. Hawthorn, C. S. Belshaw, and S. M. Jamieson, *The Indians of British Columbia: A Study of Contemporary Social Adjustment* (Berkeley and Los Angeles: University of California Press, 1958), p. 22.

And other factors may have considerable pertinence, in explaining why the Wilsons have moved farther towards the White man's way than have both the Gordons and the Harrys. Barnett's study of innovation documents the many complex factors that must be taken into account to explain why some individuals accept new ways more easily than others.[3] In the light of his considerations, it might be suggested that Mrs. Wilson's previous marriage to a White man may be one of the most pertinent factors making for her "disaffection" with the Indian way in household living. Also, it may be that the daughters, progressing through the town's high school and associating with the town's White children are partially responsible for new tastes introduced into the Wilson home. It may have been the daughters, for instance, who—between the summers of 1954 and 1957—brought a new look into the Wilson living room. Whereas in 1954 the furniture had been arranged Indian-style around the edges of the room, in 1957 the arrangement was more in accord with the usual pattern in a White home. The furniture hugged the walls less rigidly, and a large coffee table in front of the sofa definitely projected into the center space. It must be remembered that neither the Harrys nor the Gordons had children who had gone to the town high school.

Still other considerations come to mind. Recency of the infiltration of the White strain, for instance, may be one of the factors making for the Wilson nonconformism with the Indian way. It must be noted that Mr. Wilson's connections as an Indian go no further back than his father on the male side, since his grandfather was a White man; whereas in the Harry family the Indian kinship groups, with all their Indian customs, span many more generations. Gordon family informants were a little vague as to when their White ancestor entered the scene.

Another consideration involves the urge for prestige. Both Bill Gordon and Paul Harry could claim a certain amount of prestige in purely Indian terms which Mr. Wilson did not have.

---

3. Homer G. Barnett, *Innovation: The Basis of Cultural Change* (New York: McGraw-Hill Book Company, 1953).

Bill Gordon, descended from a line of chiefs, was still called "chief," and still functioned somewhat in the manner of the old household headman. Mr. Harry, though not descended from chiefs, was eldest son of a prominent Indian constable and held a position that commanded some respect because of his knowledge of old ritual secrets and ways. Mrs. Wilson herself was the informant who had told me that Mr. Harry was one of the gravediggers, and there was no derogation in her voice as she explained that he knew the "special things" to say before digging a grave. And in the summer of 1957 one of Mrs. Wilson's highly acculturated daughters reported to me in a matter-of-fact way that she and her parents had attended some of the local dances held in the Harry home that winter. Her tone seemed to suggest that naturally this was the thing to do, and there was no implication that they had found it unpleasant to leave their spotless house to sit down in the Harry "camp."

Mr. Wilson, on the other hand, was neither "chief" nor ritualist, though his father was a man who seemed to have had some prominence on the reserve and one of his brothers was elected chief in a neighboring band. The need to compete for prestige in any terms that he could find it may have led him to an opportunistic straddling of the two cultural patterns, Indian and White.

Still other determining factors might come to light, in an exhaustive study. Suffice it to point out here that change is proceeding at different rates and in different ways in Camas families for a variety of complex reasons. We may be sure, however, that at the heart of the reasons, whatever they are, can be found the universal striving for a feeling of satisfaction in interpersonal relations, a feeling that the daily round is being lived in a way that has meaning and provides for each individual, as Barnett has said, some system for "maintaining himself as an integrated, continuing entity, the same now as in the past and continuing into the future." [4]

4. Ibid., p. 113.

6

Family and Community Life

THE CROWDED, CLUTTERED HOUSEHOLD

We have indicated that it is common to find the houses on the reserve treated as temporary camps—abandoned in summer, and furnished and functioning in a way reminiscent of the past; that it is common, too, to find the houses occupied by more than the conjugal unit of mother, father, and children. Probably no single explanation for the crowded, cluttered household living encompasses all the cases. It may be more fruitful to think of a variety of explanations entering into the whole complex web of conditions and values underlying the present phenomena of Camas household life.

Let us consider, in the first place, the possibility that the crowded, camp-like way of life represents the persistence of old values and customs that have remained the same because there has not been sufficient economic and social impetus for change. The one-family houses that have been built for the Indian and now stand about the reserve in imitation of the White man's conjugal homes are, indeed, in a sense only an imitation, something capped down over a set of conditions unlike those that lie behind the neat, one-family houses of the residents of the town. As we know, it is the industrialization of our society that has broken up the more extended-family way of life of our rural ancestors. The conjugal family dwelling has become the logical unit in a society where both social and geographical mobility are possible and necessary within the highly competitive occupational framework, and where rapid social change has separated the generations widely, making for incompatibility of values and attitudes. The one-family dwelling itself has taken on the function of symbolizing the family's status, which has now become highly dependent upon what the husband can achieve occupationally.

Our Vancouver Island town is a part of the industrial society and its values. In the Chamber of Commerce brochure, the photographs of the little homes standing in the midst of their well-kept lawns and gardens plainly say, "See, even people who do not have a great deal of money can live here in a way that is comfortable and gives a very good impression."

The Camas Indian, though living on the doorstep of the town, is not really a part of its occupational and status system. The society which industrialization has built is not the society within which he lives. Until recently uneducated, and held to his own reserve if he wants to own Indian land and to reap the benefits of membership in the Indian band, he has had little opportunity for mobility in any direction, geographic, occupational, social. His status as an Indian has cut across all the other status possibilities.

The young Camas Indian with a new bride has not felt entirely free to pack up with her and move away, to try his fortune wherever a good job might beckon. His "fortune," since his birth, has been enmeshed with the life of the reserve and the provisions of the government for his welfare. Born into a band, his birthright is a per capita share of the band funds, the privilege of inheriting land on his reserve, and a share in all the Indian benefits such as certain freedoms from taxes and many other financial burdens. The Indian residence system has thus remained patrilocal, occasionally matrilocal, as in the old days. In general, the groom brings his bride into his parents' home until separate quarters can be provided in the form of a house on a corner of the parental land. That the official enfranchisement of Indian men has occurred so rarely indicates that it has not been looked upon with favor as a way of life.

True, in recent years, a few families have gone down to the States and have tried life there for at least a year or two without any official enfranchisement. This trend may be increasing and may indicate a growing restlessness with the old Indian way and the tie to the reserve, a growing readiness to try a freer, more mobile way of life. In the summer of 1957, I learned that at least three families who had lived in Village I in 1954 had gone to the States and had been there over a year. Another family was living in Vancouver for a period.

It may be expected that as the younger Indian becomes educated and increasingly turns his back on his parents' old beliefs, he may seek geographic mobility more and more, and a competitive place on the White man's status ladder, if he is permitted to. His one-family home, neatly painted, will become in reality more of a home for the conjugal family. It will serve less and less as a temporary shelter or camp; the curtains at the windows and the chrome-trimmed dinette sets will advertise new values and the wish to be a part of the White man's world. But at present for many members of the band the old values obtain. At the base of status has been the concept of giving and spending, not the notion of enriching oneself. Status has had nothing to do with keeping up a house. As we have already mentioned, even the young chief in 1954 was living with his wife and four children in a wretched three-room shack, cluttered almost beyond belief.

Of course, there are other considerations. The camp-like "housekeeping" may represent more than merely the persistence of old values and old habits of living. In some cases, at least, it may be partially the result of the actual physical difficulties involved in keeping house for a large family of children in a crude dwelling built without closets, shelves, laundry room, or running water.

The chief in 1954 spoke very disparagingly of even the new houses the agency was helping to provide, mainly because of the lack of a room for the women to use for laundry. It may be that the officials in the agency have not been sufficiently aware of how important an item the laundry is in an Indian woman's life. Whatever the conditions of living, the clothes get washed, and washed frequently. The Camas Indian retains his old values on personal cleanliness, and though young children are allowed to become very dirty, it was certainly my impression that older children, adolescents, and adults usually present a clean outer appearance to the world. I did not once see an adult Indian, anywhere on the reserve, whose clothing did not appear to be clean. My observations, however, did not include a great many members of the band who were away berrying.

There is no place in the usual crude Indian house to put either clean or dirty clothing for six, eight, or ten people. I have described the solution old Mrs. Bill Gordon came to: the mountains of clothing in that overpopulated house were simply tossed onto the rumpled beds. In another home, occupied by a man and wife aged thirty-four and twenty-eight, their own five children (one an eight-month-old baby), and a small niece taken in because her own mother had "gone wild," a small bedroom was used almost as a bin to hold clothing. On the day I visited the home, I noted that this room had been filled with what appeared to be clothing and rags to a depth of about three feet. The wife of this household was full of complaints about the difficulties of her life, and said again and again that she would like to "fix the house up." According to her own report, she and her husband and children had lived in Washington for about four years and had found life much better there. They had had a "nice house" with running water, and her husband had been able to make seventeen dollars a day at logging, compared with the twelve dollars a day she said he made here. She had had friends among the White people there, whereas here, as she said, "the White people don't like the Indians much and I can't blame them, because of the way the Indians here drink." This was her story. The only part of it that I could really verify was the lack of running water in the house. Every bit of water, for washing, cooking, cleaning, or drinking, had to be "packed" in pails from a water tap at the back of the house next door.

In another household (in Village III) occupied by one of the oldest couples of the band and their thirteen-year-old grandchild, it is remarkable that the housekeeping was managed as well as it was, considering that the house was on a hill, and all water had to be carried in pails from the river down beyond the steep hill's slope. This house, whose living room was furnished in the Big House style, with a few bare wooden benches and chairs and a couch around the edges of the room, seemed to me extremely cluttered but not necessarily dirty. A glimpse into the kitchen revealed a table so loaded with articles that it suggested the Mad Hatter's teaparty; a glimpse into a small dark bedroom gave the impression of something completely scrambled and tousled.

The appearance of clutter in still another home, this one in Village II, was due mainly to a crude attempt to find places to put all the clothing necessary for a family consisting of mother, father, and seven children ranging from three months to fourteen years. Wires had been strung across the living room to hold clothing; a small shelf-like arrangement had been built against one wall, on and off of which various piles of clothes and cloths sagged and fell; clothes were hanging at all angles from all sorts of nails in the walls. Sweaters lay on the chairs and couch; boots and shoes had been pushed under the beds. The general impression was of three-dimensional space in which the object had been to try to fill that space from ceiling to floor. All water for this home was carried from the river, which flowed very near the house; washing was done in a machine operated by a gas engine.

The inadequacy of the houses built for the Indians was recognized by the agency, even in 1957 when many new homes were going up. But it was considered better to help provide reasonably good accommodations for the many than very good ones for the few. Pertinent also to this question of housing may be two beliefs about the Indian which the superintendent expressed to me: that giving him too much removes his own incentive to work and that he is used to living from hand to mouth and is satisfied with a low level. This does not mean that the agency was indifferent to such basic hardships as lack of running water and electricity. Between 1954 and 1957 great improvements were made in the form of electricity everywhere and city water mains for Village II, which formerly had been entirely dependent upon river water.

Houses were built according to two or three basic architectural plans which the agency made available. A cash contribution toward lumber was made by the agency and also sometimes by the band fund. Indian carpenters were hired to assist the owner with the actual construction. It was never the agency's intention to finish up a house and present it to the Indian complete with such extras as built-in cupboards, bathrooms, or laundry rooms. An Indian who might want a bathroom in his home could have one, but would have to ask for a loan for the purpose of installing it. Indians who had income levels high enough to provide better housing with their own resources were decidedly in the minority.

Within this general picture of admittedly difficult housing, we cannot escape the differing dynamic assessments—to use MacIver's term [1]—the differing valuations which led some families at least to sort out their clothes and hang them on wires, while others made out in completely scrambled interiors. Consider old Mrs. Bill Gordon and her daughter Margaret in the adjoining room. Perhaps it was partly because she placed such a value on spending her days at the beer parlor that the older woman allowed her home to become such a shambles. Somehow Margaret, living next door in the same house, had learned to value the use of a chest of drawers and a curtained-off corner for a closet, making for a much neater interior. Indeed, the value placed on drinking may be one of the big factors accounting for the devaluation of neat housekeeping, in the cases of many of those women known to be heavy drinkers. Mrs. Paul Harry in her home cluttered with cans, shoes, bottles, papers, and rags, may be another such case.

1. R. M. MacIver, *Social Causation* (Boston: Ginn and Company, 1942).

THE WOMEN OF THE HOUSE: PERSISTENCE OF OLD ROLES

We have offered several possible reasons, or combinations of reasons, some of them hinging upon value assessments, why many of the Camas households practically belie the name and stand about on the reserve in a state of disorder, periodic abandonment, and crowded living that tends to offend the White neighbor. Even one of the superintendents, working for a temporary period on this reserve, admitted, "I have to stand outside when I go around to their houses, they're so cluttered and dirty." But there is still another consideration to be explored, one that has an important bearing on the household situation. The Indian woman's concept of her role as housekeeper, wife, and mother is central in the picture.

As we have already indicated, it would be a mistake to visualize each Indian home as a conjugal family unit. It would be equally misleading to picture the wife in the household as brought up to carry the responsibilities that the wives of the town generally carry, or even as conceiving of her role in the same way. It must be remembered that the older Camas Indian woman is only one step removed from the days of the Big House, the days when the old Indian culture was intact. The oldest grandmothers alive at the present time (there are several in their eighties) actually grew up under a regime that was only just beginning to feel the impact of the White man's entry. These old grandmothers, as young girls, probably never dreamed that marriage could or should mean the complete responsibility for household management or for care of children. The life their own grandmothers and mothers had led them to expect was one in which the newly married bride fitted into a large household, where there were numerous competent older people to take charge of the daily affairs. Even the children were left more in the care of the grandparents than of the mother, since the older people were the repositories of wisdom, the teachers, while the younger women were needed for trips to the berry fields and for clam digging on the beaches.

Numerous incidents could be cited of household situations today in which the grandmother is still functioning in the important role of manager and rearer of children. When the young daughter-in-law and son move out to a home of their own—and generally they do, eventually—they are facing a situation with which they may be ill prepared at first to cope. There has not been a long tradition of training girls in the art of running a house on their own or in caring for children. In fact, one of the Catholic priests reported that the young couples he marries simply stare at him when he tells them they must bring up their *own* children, since things are not what they were fifty years ago. "At first when I say that to the young people, they don't get it, but gradually they're catching on. The grandparents have quite a grasp on them, though."

Take, for example, our young mother in household 37 in Village I. In the summer of 1954 this home was a truly conjugal home, occupied by only the husband and wife and their baby. But when the bride first moved into the house, it was the home of the parents-in-law and their two sons. The young "bride" (not legally married until eight months after the first baby was born) gave birth to her infant there when she was not quite seventeen. According to her own report, the baby was really reared by the grandmother. She could not answer my specific questions about time and method of toilet training, for instance. "His grandmother taught him. I only fed him and washed his clothes." The extended family group occupied the house until the baby became a boy of six. About that time the second son married, and the grandparents along with the second son and his wife moved to a new home built with agency help. They took with them the six-year-old boy, to rear him as their own child.

I asked the young mother how she felt about having her little boy live with the grandparents. "I don't mind. They treat him well, and they only had two sons." This reply suggests the concept, which I often heard expressed, that grandparents would be lonely if they did not have children with them. As one of the workers in the Indian Office explained it, "The Indians are very generous with their children, you might say. Generous about giving children to people who don't have any. They think it's terrible for people to be without children. They wouldn't think of leaving grandparents without some young children around." In Village I alone I knew of four other households where at least one child in the family was a grandchild, living with a grandparent couple as though he were their own. In a fifth family, a distantly related "niece" and "nephew" of the husband had been reared from birth as the couple's own and only children. In a sixth, one of a pair of twins had been given to an aunt in Victoria, who had no children. In several other cases, grandparents were keeping children during the summer months while the parents were off in the States picking berries, or—in a few cases—fishing.

It is probably not to be doubted that the grandparents who took in grandchildren to rear as their own really did want the children very much. After all, a Camas Indian woman, married at seventeen or eighteen or even younger, becomes a grandmother at an early age. But it is likely, too, that the custom also reveals the persistence of roles and concepts that were integral to the old family structure of the Big House days.

In other ways as well, the older Camas Indians today tend to retain some of the family functions and roles that were theirs in the past. I heard from both the priest and the workers in the agency that there are still attempts made by the older generation to arrange marriages for the young people, always with economic transactions involved. The priest told of a case in which the girl's family had already been paid one hundred dollars before the affair came to his attention. The girl sought him out in distress, since her parents were trying to force her into this marriage. The priest took her to one of the other villages, where she spent the night with cousins, and in the meantime he talked to the parents and managed to prevent the forcible action. "When I marry a young couple," he said, "I always ask them, 'Are you really *free* to marry?' "

In spite of such cases, however, the old institution of arranged marriage has been on the way out ever since the fall of the potlatching system, and this may have some bearing on the present household situation and role of the wife. In the old culture, it will be remembered, marriage was never based on personal choice; it was always arranged by the parents, and was calculated to further social prestige. A good match was one which increased the desirable social connections of both parties, linking families who could offer protection and hospitality outside of the local village, and who could be of economic help to each other in the great accumulations necessary for potlatching. Today personal choice is becoming the major consideration, and it is likely to be personal choice based on personal attraction.

It seems possible—though one can only offer this as a tentative hypothesis, because of the limited data available—that this tenuous basis for marriage may bear some functional relation to the emphasis many wives place today not only on their own personal appearance—much more than on the appearance of their homes—but also on pleasing their husbands by trying to do whatever they wish, even though it may involve neglect of home and children. Not only can husbands and wives part and "remarry" today as easily as in the past—Catholic church and White man's legal strictures notwithstanding—but there are no longer the old compelling considerations of family advantage to help cement the union. The woman has nothing but her own choice and her husband's to hold the marriage together. So, if she wishes to stay with her mate, she keeps herself attractive for him and does his bidding. She puts her hair up in bobby pins, gives herself home permanents, or gets them in the beauty parlors in the town, and wears a good deal of sparkling jewelry. There she is, dressed up in her brooches and earrings and a flowered print dress, all ready to go out to the beer parlor with her husband in the early afternoon. The Indian Health Services nurse happens along and finds her thus, just putting some milk into a thermos for the baby, who is to be left in the care of the other children. Querying the mother as to why she is going off like this, leaving her children, she is told, "But my husband wants me to."

That the woman's position is theoretically inferior to the man's, just as, in the old days, the man was the one who had the greater status, was evidenced to me in a number of ways. At the Shaker services, it is the men who go up to the altar first, to put their money into the collection plate; the women follow when the men have all returned to their places. When women go to sell their sweaters at the store on the highway, or trade the sweaters in for groceries, they are invariably accompanied by their husbands, who apparently wish to be there to see that the deal is satisfactorily made. Sometimes the husbands come along when the errand is merely one of buying groceries, but when the couple leave the store, the woman is always the one who carries the packages.

The most dramatic illustration of the male dominance, however, is in the wife beating (also an old custom), which the Indian Health Services doctor and nurse independently reported as not only very common, but something the wife expects, takes submissively, and does not resent. "Why," the doctor said, "they just think that's every man's right and privilege. And the women would think their men were a little soft if they didn't beat them. They take it for granted." But he went on to say that in his opinion "the Indian men and women know more about real love than we White folks do. They don't live together as man and wife unless they really care for each other. Not like our marriages, where we marry to make a show, have a nice home, and stick together regardless of how we feel."

The cluttered house; the grimy children racing in and out; the mother emerging for a trip to the beer parlor with her husband, hair curled in the White woman's fashion—this household scene could be taken as a symbol of the pattern of life that has taken shape for at least some of the Indian population during this period of transition, as the old established basis for marriage has fallen away, while the grandmother, the reserve, and the government have remained. Caught between the old and the new, the woman has not yet learned the household way of life which the White neighbor carries on with ease. And it must be remembered that the old way still may make very good sense to the Indian woman. Behind her values and choices today are old habits of association: marriage in the old culture always was companionable, and men and women always were present together at important functions. Why should the woman today choose to let her husband go off to the beer parlor without her? And why should it necessarily be supposed that the obligation of caring for children could compete with other wifely obligations and ways which may seem paramount to the woman herself?

That we are not speaking of all the Indian women should be self-evident. There are those like Mrs. Wilson and Margaret Gordon and others we have mentioned who assume highly responsible roles as housekeepers and rearers of children, and furthermore help hold the family together economically with their sweater sales. The Indian sweater trade, almost exclusively in the hands of the women, is a forty thousand dollar industry [2] in which the majority of at least the middle-aged and older women have a hand, just as in the old days all had a hand in blanket weaving. In fact, it may very well be that in many a home the dishes accumulate and the clutter piles up partly because the women of the house feel the pressure to finish that next sweater.

It is probably true, also, that this dependable income accruing through the woman's skill in handiwork makes her role somewhat more satisfying to her than the man's is to him today, despite the many transitional problems we have discussed. In addition, as each day goes by, there is always work at hand for the woman to do, whether or not she does it thoroughly, whether or not she understands or cares about the niceties of housekeeping. There are always people depending on her for preparation of food and for laundering of clothes. She is needed.

And if she seeks income through taking a job as dishwasher in a restaurant in town or in a sanatorium, this probably does not introduce a radically disrupting element into the family life or into the expectations regarding female role, since always

2. As reported in local Chamber of Commerce brochure.

the Indian woman had considerable autonomy. She pursued her specialized skills as the man did; and her daily "work" often took her long distances from the home, to gather roots and berries and rushes or to dig clams on the beach.

Her roles have not changed greatly since the old days, nor has her status within the Indian community diminished. It is when she begins comparing her domestic lot with that of the women of the town, or when she attempts to take on occupational roles traditionally allocated only to the White working woman, that her status suffers.

MARRIAGES

How Stable Are They?

I have just mentioned that parting and remarrying appear to be as easy today as in the past. Does this mean that the households are occupied by a constantly shifting series of partners in search of that "real love" referred to by the doctor? And if this is the case, what are the implications in terms of broken homes for the children?

Study of the Village I band list, supplemented by my knowledge of individuals and households there, gives a reasonably accurate clue to the situation and reveals that marriages—or unions, as they might better be called—are more stable than might be imagined. As table 1 indicates, 18.1 percent, or nineteen of the one hundred and five "married" individuals whose homes were in the village in the summer of 1954 were known

TABLE 1

VILLAGE I: DISTRIBUTION OF MARITAL UNIONS, 1954
(Total $N = 105$)

Union	Number	Percent
One only	79	75.2
More than one	19	18.1
No data	7	6.7

to have had more than one union. Of these, only two men and two women had been "married" more than twice. The two men had each had four unions, the two women three. Some information was lacking on seven of the one hundred and five individuals, mainly because they had come in from other bands and were not registered on the Camas lists. Of these seven, I think it possible that at least four might have had previous unions. This would raise the percentage of married individuals who had had more than one union to 20.2 percent.

Unions referred to here, of course, are all those in which a couple live together as man and wife, and all those resulting in children. The census is interested in the marital status of each member of the band because of the bearing on band membership and privileges, and also is interested in recording all births and registering each child in some band—in his father's if the paternity is "acknowledged" (that is, if the father signs the birth record) and in his mother's if the paternity is only "alleged," or reported by the mother.

TABLE 2

VILLAGE I: DISTRIBUTION OF MARITAL UNIONS BY AGE GROUP, 1954
(Total $N = 105$)

Union	Up to 30 ($N = 32$) Number	Percent	31 to 50 ($N = 35$) Number	Percent	51 and Up ($N = 38$) Number	Percent
One only	30	93.8	26	74.3	23	60.6
More than one	1	3.1	4	11.4	14	36.8
No data	1	3.1	5	14.3	1	2.6

A breakdown of unions by ages (table 2) shows that the young (up to 30) and middle-aged (31 to 50) couples have been by no means carrying on a shifting marital life. It is the older individuals (51 and up) who look back on a life that has, for fourteen of them at least, built up to a second or third marriage, after death of one spouse or a marriage that did not work. Sex differences, as shown in table 3, are not striking, particularly in view

TABLE 3

VILLAGE I: DISTRIBUTION OF MARITAL UNIONS BY AGE GROUP AND BY SEX, 1954
(Total $N = 51$ men and 54 Women)

| | UP TO 30 ||||| 31 TO 50 ||||| 51 AND UP ||||
| | MEN ($N = 14$) || WOMEN ($N = 18$) || MEN ($N = 15$) || WOMEN ($N = 20$) || MEN ($N = 22$) || WOMEN ($N = 16$) ||
UNION	Number	Percent	Number	Percent	Number	Percent	Number	Percent	Number	Percent	Number	Percent
One only	13	92.9	17	94.4	12	80.0	14	70.0	15	68.2	8	50.0
More than one	0	0.0	1	5.6	1	6.7	3	15.0	7	31.8	7	43.8
No data	1	7.1	0	0.0	2	13.3	3	15.0	0	0.0	1	6.2

TABLE 4

VILLAGE I: DISTRIBUTION OF MARITAL DISSOLUTIONS, 1954
(Total $N = 51$ Men and 54 Women)

	Men	Women	Totals
Separation	5	7	12
Divorce	0	0	0
Death	5	7	12
No data	3	3	6
TOTALS	13	17	30

Includes cases of individuals separated or widowed, who have had only one union.

of the small numbers in each grouping and the lack of data on some cases. As indicated in table 4, death has been probably as important a cause of dissolution of marriage as separation.

One of the conclusions that can be drawn from this data is that the old system of relationships persists, though the basis for marriage has changed. Just as in the old days marriage was valued, so it is today, though shorn of its old significance as a prestige-enhancing mechanism. The present-day Camas Indian seldom lives long without a mate.

Among all the residents of Village I, there was only one older man, aged forty-seven, listed as a single man throughout all the band lists from 1931 on. And actually there is some reason to believe that he may not have been single, at least in 1954, but may have had a common-law wife whose name was not noted beside his in the list because there were no offspring and because no one in the Indian Office happened to pencil in a notation to the effect that the man was living with a woman. There were only two other men over twenty-five, known by me to be residents, who were listed as single, and in such cases there is always some room for doubt. The name of a common-law wife from another band would not automatically be listed with the common-law husband; and until recently even in cases of acknowledged paternity, the children of such unions might be listed only in the mother's band list.

Other single individuals in Village I included one widower,

a man who lost his wife in 1952 and had not yet taken another mate, and three women, widowed or separated, who had not remarried. Two of these were very old women, one of them widowed in 1954 at the age of seventy-one; the third had just parted from her husband in 1954. Among the younger women there were none over twenty-five who were still single.

The question might be raised: How can one be sure that all the unions resulting in births of children should be considered "marriages"? How many of these births were illegitimate, according to our understanding of the term, and in no way indicated that the mother and father had lived together as in a marriage? The answer to this is that there are several clues, the most important being some first-hand knowledge of the families, secondly the band list itself. Often there has been a legal marriage, in which case there is almost always a notation to this effect; and usually in the case of a common-law union of long standing, the man and wife are shown together, and the long lists of children accruing under their names are evidence of a continuing relationship.

My study of the Village I data leads me to believe that of all recorded births in families of 1954 residents, only three, involving three different mothers, may have occurred outside the pattern of marriage. There were a number of cases, however, involving eight individuals, or four couples, in which marriage did not take place until shortly before the first child was born. It is impossible to accurately reconstruct the meaning of this, without case study material, in a culture where the White man's legal marriage ceremony has not been considered an indispensable preliminary to marriage. As indicated in table 5, though only sixteen individuals (15.2 percent of the "married" individuals) were living in common-law unions in 1954, a total of 47.6 percent had lived in a common-law union at some time during their lives. This includes sixteen couples who lived together as common-law man and wife before a legal ceremony was performed. Some of these had lived together many years, and had had many children before the union was made legal.

A study was made of Village II data, relying on band list in-

TABLE 5

VILLAGE I: DISTRIBUTION OF COMMON-LAW AND LEGAL UNIONS, 1954
(Total $N = 105$)

Union	Number	Percent
COMMON-LAW		
Living common-law	16	15.2
Legally married, but lived together first as common-law man and wife [a]	32	30.5
Legally married, but have had common-law relations with previous spouses	2	1.9
TOTALS	50	47.6
LEGAL ONLY		
Legally married only	48	45.7
DATA LACKING		
Legally married; no data on common-law	5	4.8
Probably outside pattern of marriage [b]	1	0.9
No data	1	0.9

a. Includes four couples not legally married until six months or less before birth of first child.
b. Two additional individuals believed to have had children outside the pattern of marriage are now known to be either legally married or living common-law and are included in other categories.

formation for 1953, since notations for 1954 had not yet been completed by the agency. Results are roughly comparable, but admittedly cannot be considered as accurate as those presented for Village I, since my firsthand knowledge of the Village II families was less complete; nor can it be considered that the figures refer in a literal sense only to the residents of Village II. I excluded families known or believed by me to reside elsewhere, even though their names appeared on the Village II band list, but I did not have exact knowledge of residence of each family. What is important, however, is that these figures do refer to a group of one hundred and one "married" Camas Indians (or Indians who have had children), who do not reside in Village I, adjoining the town. The data show (table 6) that 21.8 percent, or twenty-two individuals out of the one hundred and one, have

TABLE 6

VILLAGE II: DISTRIBUTION OF MARITAL UNIONS, 1953
(Total $N = 101$)

Union	Number	Percent
One only	79	78.2
More than one	22	21.8

had more than one union. Of these, five men and two women have had more than two unions (in six cases, three; in once case, four). If there are inaccuracies in this overall figure of 21.8 percent, they are in the direction of a slight underestimate rather than an overestimate. Firsthand knowledge of the families might have revealed a few recent separations not yet noted in the band list, as well as some additional common-law unions.

A breakdown by ages (table 7) shows that, as in the case of Village I, the younger couples do not separate and remarry frequently. It is the older ones who accumulate the unions.

TABLE 7

VILLAGE II: DISTRIBUTION OF MARITAL UNIONS BY AGE GROUP, 1953
(Total $N = 101$)

Union	Up to 30 ($N = 32$) Number	Percent	31 to 50 ($N = 30$) Number	Percent	51 and Up ($N = 39$) Number	Percent
One only	31	96.9	24	80.0	24	61.5
More than one	1	3.1	6	20.0	15	38.5

Figures for the two villages are very similar, particularly if we assume that the four individuals on whom information was lacking in Village I actually had had a former union. All four of these cases fall in the middle-aged group (31 to 50), and would raise the percentage of 11.4 in this category to 22.9, which is very close to the 20.0 percent for Village II. Likewise, highly comparable are the results of the breakdown by sexes (table 8).

TABLE 8

Village II: Distribution of Marital Unions by Age Group and by Sex, 1953
(Total N = 52 Men and 49 Women)

Union	Up to 30 Men ($N=11$) Number	Percent	Up to 30 Women ($N=21$) Number	Percent	31 to 50 Men ($N=18$) Number	Percent	31 to 50 Women ($N=12$) Number	Percent	51 and Up Men ($N=23$) Number	Percent	51 and Up Women ($N=16$) Number	Percent
One only	11	100.0	20	95.2	15	83.3	9	75.0	14	60.9	10	62.5
More than one	0	0.0	1	4.8	3	16.7	3	25.0	9	39.1	6	37.5

MARRIAGES

TABLE 9

VILLAGE II: DISTRIBUTION OF MARITAL DISSOLUTIONS, 1953
(Total $N = 52$ Men and 49 Women)

	Men	Women	Totals
Separation	13	8	21
Divorce	2	0	2
Death	7	7	14
Other: "no father listed"	0	5	5
No data	9	2	11
TOTALS	31	22	53

Includes cases of individuals now separated or widowed, who have had only one union.

As table 9 shows, death as well as separation has been a cause of marital dissolution, just as in the case of Village I.

A new category appears, however: "no father listed." There were no such cases in Village I, among 1954 residents. These may be cases of illegitimate birth occurring outside the pattern of marriage. It seems unlikely that the absence of the names of any alleged or acknowledged fathers is due simply to error or time lag in catching up with the registration of vital statistics. In one of the cases, there is the notation, "father unknown." In the other four cases, showing the name of an infant registered along with that of a single unmarried woman, the births occurred in 1951 or 1952 or earlier, to young women between the ages of nineteen and twenty-three. A likely hypothesis, since these births took place in the spring of the year, is that these unions were among those temporary ones occurring during the annual summer trip to the berry fields.

There are at least three additional cases in Village II of unions that appear to have occurred outside the pattern of marriage. In one case, a man had a child by his deceased brother's wife, while he was also having children by his own wife. This recalls old custom. In the second case, a man listed as legal father of a large family appears in the list as "alleged father" of a child born four months after his wife's first child, to a woman of

FAMILY AND COMMUNITY LIFE

another village who has had numerous unions. The third case is that of a man who had a child by one woman two months after he was married to another. He later separated from his legal wife and took the first woman as a common-law wife.

TABLE 10

VILLAGE II: DISTRIBUTION OF COMMON-LAW AND LEGAL UNIONS, 1953
(Total $N = 101$)

Union	Number	Percent
COMMON-LAW		
Living common-law	16	15.8
Legally married, but lived together first as common-law man and wife [a]	33	32.7
Legally married, but have had common-law relations with previous spouses	5	4.9
Have lived common-law; no partner in 1953	2	2.0
Have lived common-law; no data on later unions	1	1.0
TOTALS	57	56.4
LEGAL ONLY		
Legally married only	31	30.7
DATA LACKING		
Legally married; no data on common-law	2	2.0
Probably outside pattern of marriage [b]	5	5.0
No data	6	5.9

a. Includes three couples not legally married until three months before birth of first child.
b. Three additional individuals believed to have had children outside the pattern of marriage are now known to be either legally married or living common-law and are included in other categories.

As table 10 indicates, common-law unions have been somewhat more frequent for Village II than for Village I (compare 56.4 percent with 47.6 percent; not statistically significant, however, at the five percent level of confidence). It would be interesting in a further study to explore the hypothesis that there is a functional relationship between residence in or near the town, and the smaller percentage of common-law unions for Village I.

The prevalence of common-law unions among the Camas, to the extent of approximately half of the married population at one time or another during their married lives, calls for explanation.

Common-Law Marriage

It might seem that where the Catholic church has been active in its missionary work for eighty years, the church's beliefs about marriage might have been more generally adopted. Possibly it is partly because of the tolerant attitude of the church toward the Indians in this respect that the principles have not taken hold any more than they have. "It's partly old custom, and partly just human nature," one of the priests said to me in discussing the prevalence of common-law marriage.

He went on to offer two other contributory explanations, however—both of them no doubt pertinent in at least some of the cases. He pointed out that some of the common-law unions occur among the Shakers, who have no marriage rite. He also was under the impression that a legal ceremony could interfere with a couple's living arrangements, and is for that reason sometimes circumvented. He cited the case of a boy he had known from up the coast who was living on the Camas Reserve with a common-law wife and her people, an arrangement all of them wanted. The priest believed, and it may be that the boy also erroneously believed, that if he had married legally he would have had to return to his own reserve and take his wife with him. Actually, as the superintendent pointed out to me, this does not always have to happen. A women upon marriage must theoretically dispose of any land she may own in the band of her birth, but the band council can and often does give permission for a couple to reside on the wife's reserve rather than the husband's. Bill Gordon's daughter Margaret is a case in point.

Several other explanations, from other individuals, offer further pertinent leads and point up the fact that the common-law marriage practice is one of many dimensions and that probably no one motive can be stretched to cover all the cases.

Still another explanation involving circumvention of the ceremony for practical purposes was given by the superintendent who was on temporary duty during the early part of the summer of 1954. In his opinion, the government's practice of periodically distributing band fund interest moneys has encouraged the common-law marriage custom. According to him, a woman who might be receiving an interest distribution sum of perhaps twenty-five dollars in the band of her birth might want to try to retain this, if marrying into a band where the interest accruing to each individual was much less. In order not to forfeit her twenty-five dollars, as she would if she legally married into the other band, she simply lives in a common-law union and continues drawing her money.

Intensive case studies of common-law unions would have to be made in order to ferret out the extent of this practice. It may be that the superintendent in question did know of a few such cases. Other officials in the Indian Office pointed out, however, that it works both ways. A woman sometimes finds herself marrying into a band where the interest distribution sum is greater than in her own band. In this case, legal marriage is an advantage to her.

I have studied the data on the eight Village I couples now living in common-law unions and doubt that this explanation relative to interest distribution has much pertinence in these particular cases. True, the wife of one of the couples has received interest distributions from the band of her birth, which I shall call Douglas Bay, more recently than she would have received them from the Camas, if legally married, since the government is discouraging the practice and the last distribution for the Camas was in 1951. The most recent for Douglas Bay was in 1953. However, this particular common-law union was entered into twenty-five years ago. A study of the Camas distribution moneys for the past twenty-five years, compared with the sums for Douglas Bay, would be interesting but would not in itself provide a definitive clue, since there are many other reasons for the common-law practice.

In the case of another couple in Village I living in a common-law union of long standing, the wife would have profited from interest distribution in recent years if she had married into her husband's band, not the Camas, since the most recent distribution in his band was in 1954. This is the case of a man permitted to reside in Village I, though theoretically a member of another band, because of ancestral land and connections among the Camas. He cannot own land, however, without transferring membership. Four—or possibly five—of our Village I common-law couples are unable to marry, simply because one member of the couple is already legally married to someone else. In the eighth case, both the husband and wife belong to the Camas Band, so the interest distribution question has no pertinence.

An entirely different type of explanation for the common-law marriage custom was given by Bill Gordon's daughter Margaret, who clearly was thinking of the young people today, perhaps of her own troublesome seventeen-year-old daughter, when she said: "It's just that the kids try to be the boss these days. They don't listen to their parents any more. In the old days everyone got married Indian fashion." It should be made clear that the old Indian wedding ceremony—a costly affair—is seldom performed any more. The last one, according to the priest, was held in 1951 for a Village II bride and groom, who also had the legal Catholic ceremony. As far as I could ascertain, couples who enter into common-law unions today simply begin living together, without a ceremony of any kind. Actually, this may have been the custom even in the early days, among the commoners. Margaret, daughter of a line of chiefs, may not have been aware of this.

Another Indian, expressing his opinions on marriage and separation, stated what may represent the point of view of many of the older Indians. This fifty-nine-year-old man, married both Indian fashion and by the Catholic church to his present wife at least twenty-five years ago, and apparently devoted to her and to his children and grandchildren, had a common-law union with another woman before his legal marriage. Speaking about the old Indian custom, he said: "The Indians used to just separate after two or three years if they found they were not suited, and find someone else. We thought it worked out well that way. Today people can't get remarried or divorced, because they are Catholics, so they just separate and live with someone else if they're not getting along." He implied not only that the common-law marriage custom today represents the persistence of an old system of marriage relationships and values, but that the Indian is an individual who does as he thinks best, and is not to be dominated by the legal strictures of the White man. This attitude is possibly at the very core of most of the common-law practice today.

Children and Broken Homes

We have raised the question of the impact on the children of the Camas marriage structure. If today eighteen to twenty-two percent of the married population have had more than one union, what does this mean in terms of children growing up without their fathers or mothers in the home?

In Village I in 1954 there were five—possibly six—households where there were such children under the ages of sixteen. In all but one of these households—that in which an eleven-year-old girl was living alone with her mother—there were grandparents or an aunt and uncle at the head of the household, and the children were experiencing family life. Take the case of Bill Gordon's daughter Phyllis. In the summer of 1954 the Gordons were caring for the five children she had had by a man who, though acknowledging paternity, had never married Phyllis and had left her. In addition, there was a sixth child she had had by a Mexican—whether he had ever lived with her as in a marriage was not ascertained—and a seventh by a third man she later married. The heads of this household were definitely the grandfather and grandmother, not daughter Phyllis, though she lived there; and as we know already, there were numerous other relatives finding shelter under the same roof.

What emotional deprivation "fatherless" children experience, within the framework of this kind of extended family living, psychologists know little about. It seems plausible that in the Camas situation, where grandparents not only take over but are still so often *expected* to take over the care of young children, a "fatherless" home may have a much less damaging impact on the children than it may be expected to have in our own culture. Within the framework of Camas life, fatherless children who are being brought up by grandparents look around them and see many other households where grandparents are the child rearers, temporarily or permanently, for one reason or another. Also, within this climate the mother who hands her children over to the grandparents, either because her husband has left her or she has left him, or because she wants to remarry into another band, may have not only fewer conflicts about what she is doing, but a less intense relation with the children to start with. Even if she remains in the house with them and the grandparents, what conflicts she has may be felt in somewhat attenuated form, since there are so many people to receive the impact of them.

Indeed, there are other types of household disruption which may be harder on the Camas children than the disruption which is a consequence of broken marriage. I refer to two types of household disorganization which the Camas have experienced only in modern times—disruptions due to tuberculosis and to drinking.

During the summer of 1954, one father and one mother from Village I families were in the tuberculosis hospital thirty-five miles away. Other cases, necessitating long hospitalization, came to my attention in 1957. Of course, in such cases there are usually relatives who help with the care of children, just as when parents separate. Or the children may be cared for the year around by the Kuper Island boarding school. This does not, however, eliminate worry and concern over a hospitalized parent.

Perhaps even more serious are the cases of those parents who separate periodically because of conflicts arising over drinking. In such cases the children are subjected to the conflicts and experience temporary disruptions of their home life. As Margaret described her own situation: "My husband has been a drinker. Once we went down to Seattle to live, because I thought this old house was causing my children to be sick all the time. But my husband got to drinking so bad down in Seattle—he'd get so mad—that I left him and came back here. But he followed me. He's not quite so bad now, but still he drinks too much." All of this was said to me in the presence of the children.

There were at least two other Village I couples who periodically separated because of the excessive drinking of either the husband or wife. Both of these couples lived in nuclear family homes. In a fourth case where drinking had broken up a home, a grandmother had stepped in early and had reared a child of the drinking father almost from birth. "I raised her from one month old. Her father took to too much drinking, that's why. He's in Yakima, some place like that. The mother is off in Washington somewhere, too. She has more kids than just this one."

It is possible, of course, that even this kind of home disruption, made up of temporary separations and the "mad" stormings of a drunken parent, may not have the same impact on the Camas child that comparable situations might have on our own children. Even when the Camas parents separate, it may be within the framework of the band and the reserve and the widespread network of kinfolk. And when the drunken parent storms, it is unlikely that he becomes brutal toward his children. It is the wife who expects and takes the beatings. The gentle treatment of Camas children by their parents and other elders is everywhere attested to.

These children, too, it must be remembered, live in a setting where they see and share in all sides of the lives of their parents to a much greater extent than the children of the town probably do. Crowded in their homes, they see and hear; and there is little attempt to hide anything from them. An open box of sanitary napkins may lie in full view on a shelf in the main room of the house, where children of all ages mill around; anything and everything is talked about in the presence of the children; and a child even as young as seven can look you squarely in the face and explain matter-of-factly, when you refer to her "mother," "My mother left me. I live with my grandmother, but I call her Mummy."

It seems possible that such children, well knitted into the fabric of the lives of their people, and at the same time well loved, may not find the conflicts of their parents as damaging as would children in other more protected settings.

In spite of outer appearances of shabby housekeeping and loose marriage ties, then, and in spite of the prevalence of drinking and other problems that attend the breakdown of the old authority system, family life in Camas terms is by no means completely disorganized, by no means completely lacking in stable elements. On the contrary, when the present is related to the past, it can be seen that the old structure of family relationships, as well as much of the old system of household ways, endures.

LIVES OF MEN: THE CYCLE OF POVERTY AND DEPENDENCE

We have stressed so far the roles of women in the Camas households. The woman is the housekeeper and the caretaker of the children, and may appear to be the one mainly responsible for the condition of the home. But the man's role as householder, wage earner, and occupier of his plot of ground is no less significant in the total picture of household living.

Let us be sure, in the first place, that we have a clear understanding of the Camas Indian's legal status in regard to property. It should be emphasized that though he may occupy a piece of land, it is unlikely that he has a location ticket, or that the legal boundaries of his land are clear in his own mind or anyone else's, though both the band council and the agency are devoting major energies to disentangling these boundary questions at the present time. That progress is slow is probably unavoidable in a matter so clogged with old disputes and bad feeling, still active today. As Mr. Jack Harry said: "I would like to see the old ways brought back. Land boundaries aren't respected anymore. In the old days the chiefs recognized the plot of land a man took up. They must have. But that doesn't mean anything now."

Even in cases where the boundaries and title to the land are clear, an Indian's ownership is qualified. He cannot make free disposition of his property. He cannot sell to a White man, or to an Indian of another band, unless that Indian, with the permission of the band council, transfers his membership to the Camas Band. The land is reserve property, and the Indian forfeits his right to own it if he should reside away from his reserve longer than six months. The house, too, though the Indian has full right to occupy it and alter it, may not be his to own unequivocably and to pass down to his heirs. If it has been built with band fund and agency help, the agency retains an equity and can control reallocation to some extent.

Partially responsible for the poor condition that so often characterizes the house is the employment situation, which today confines the majority of Camas Indians to poverty. As workers in logging, lumbering, and longshoring, they have found employment which in some ways suits the habits and skills they have brought along with them out of the past into the modern century. It is intermittent or seasonal, thus providing breaks in the rhythm of the work year somewhat in keeping with the old Camas habits of seasonal change; it is outdoor work, also in accord with old Indian custom, and offers some excitement and challenge by way of the dangerous operations involved. Furthermore, the work calls for the skills with which the Indian seems well equipped. In the old culture, he was skilled in fishing, canoe-making, hunting. Today his manual and mechanical skills are still impressive. As one White informant, himself a logger, described it: "Out with the riggers, they'll drive the guys crazy who don't understand them. A man like Harris—you wonder if he's going to tackle the stump, and he just stands there and looks at it; and the guys say, 'Well, what are you going to do?' But he doesn't answer, just stands there and stares at the stump; but pretty soon he'll start in and then they know what to do; but he'll never talk. You have to be ninety-five percent mind reader with the Indians. But take the White men, they're apt to start to work on the stump before they've really figured out what to do, then have to undo it and start over again. The Indians are slower, but they don't make false moves."

But employment of this seasonal nature, even for the Indian who sticks with it whenever it is available, confines a man to the ranks of a casual worker and to a low level of yearly income. And, as we have seen, many do not stick with the work in spite of its many congenial features, and in spite of the fact that practically no other type of employment is available. Though it is seasonal in nature, its seasonal breaks may not always coincide with the Indian's seasonal demands. He wants to leave when the berries are ripe in the summer; and because of his independent habits he is apt to chafe under the supervision that this wage work requires. Some resent the idea of working for wages at all. As one Indian informant put it: "We Indians shouldn't have to work like this, for money. We used to have plenty to eat. If we wanted meat we'd go out and shoot a deer; and we had a few chickens, and all the fish we wanted, dried for the winter when we had our dances. Everything was good that way." So the Indian leaves his job, forfeits his unemployment insurance, and sometimes forfeits also his chances of reemployment with the companies he leaves at will.

He is unequipped by training and education for other types of work in or near the town. Tied to his reserve, he is unable to move his residence freely to other reserves where attractive work opportunities might exist; fishing in the old Indian style is no longer possible. The weirs have been removed and fishing regulations instituted, and few Indians can afford the expensive equipment that would make it possible for them to fish profitably today in the waters of the Strait. Borrowing and deficit financing are difficult, because with low income and little savings the Indian is considered a poor credit risk by banks. As has been mentioned before, farming the land is an uncongenial pursuit to the majority at present, and cooperative enterprises which might alleviate some of the economic conditions are difficult to foster in a climate where even band council members retain a sense of the separateness of the seven bands, and where cooperation outside of kin groupings runs counter to the traditional system of relationships. Thus the Camas Indian can easily become caught up in a cycle of poverty and dependence upon welfare help. His shoddy house, often crowded with needy kinfolk, is a symbol of his position as he reaches the midway point of the twentieth century, in some aspects a ward of the government, yet still activated by many of the habits and values of his past.

The yearly round of his life includes a good deal that is related to the old, as well as some features that have taken shape in recent times. Drinking in the beer parlor has become a major year-round recreational activity—characteristic, also, of the White loggers in this region, but more often in the Indian's case leading to excesses and street fighting and arrests. On Sundays the Catholic and Protestant churches draw in only a handful, while another handful, perhaps twenty-five people from the Camas Reserve, including both men and women, participate weekly in the dancing and bell ringing and singing of the Shaker services. Political activities in modern terms are minimal. Only a handful turned out for the Provincial election, when the privilege of the vote was granted in 1948. Very few are drawn into the two political organizations of the Indians of the Province— the North American Indian Brotherhood and the Native Brotherhood of British Columbia. Even the local business of the band does not bring out a large attendance at the occasional meetings called by the superintendent. According to a newspaper report of 20 December 1956, only seventy-nine of the four hundred and forty Indians eligible to vote turned out even for a special meeting called at that time to consider sale of a portion of the reserve land.

The Indian remains, as in the old days, a man who marries and stays with his family in a fairly stable union. He commutes long distances to his work in the mills and timber, returning daily, if he can, to the house with its large brood of children and grandchildren, of whom he appears to be proud and fond. Within his house—whatever it may look like to the White neighbor—and within his family and on the reserve he retains some of his old status links with the past. He is a more important man on the reserve than he is off of it. That is one of the most significant facts about his life.

In his household, in relation to his wife, he still maintains the superior position, as in the past. Some of the evidences of this, including the wife beatings which the male considers his prerogative, have been mentioned earlier. Certainly it was clear to me on my visits to the homes that the husband not only expected deference from the wife but received it. By and large, on these visits the woman retreated if the man was present. Sometimes she kept herself out of sight entirely, remaining quietly in an adjoining room. In some cases this may have been partly because she could not handle English as well as her husband could. In other cases, where the English was adequate and the wife free to chat with me when the husband was away, she clearly withdrew in the husband's presence, letting him take the initiative in the conversation.

Some of the old links of age with status endure on the Camas Reserve. The young have not made the reserve over in modern terms. Quite the contrary, young people continue to move in with their parents when they first marry, since the parents are still more able to help them than they are to help the parents; and they continue to attend the old winter dance spectacles organized and financed by the older Indians, though, as we have seen, a number are beginning to express fear and disapproval of them. The modern governing agency representing the Indians, the band council, is made up mainly of middle-aged men. The eight councillors elected in 1954 ranged in age from thirty to sixty-four, with the median falling between forty-seven and forty-nine. The chief, to be sure, was a young man of thirty-four. However, he appeared to have been elected not because of leadership qualities, but rather because he belonged to a certain important Village II family line in which chieftainship was traditional.

The older Indians still keep their names alive—their traditional Indian names, unknown to the White man—by sponsoring naming ceremonies. On these occasions, the old and their accomplishments and names are honored and lauded in a custom reminiscent of the past. Fifty-cent pieces are given as "thanks for remembering," when in the course of the laudatory speeches by the old men one of the Indian names is spoken.

In other ways, too, related to the pride and prestige dynamics of the past, the winter ceremonies as performed today offer opportunities for status satisfactions for all active participants. Indeed, it seems evident that the Camas winter ceremonies have endured with as much vitality as they have partially because they offer the Indian—to his White neighbor a marginal man, occupant of the town slum, and "just siwash"—ways and means of attaining a feeling of dignity or importance, as well as a way of continuing to function within a familiar and meaningful structure of values and relationships.

A discussion of the winter ceremonies of today, however—as well as discussion of the functions of Shakerism and drinking—will take us out of the domain of the lives of men, since these activities are shared by men and women alike, and young and old.

THE SEARCH FOR STATUS

Winter Ceremonies

In the past, it will be recalled, the winter ceremonies—whatever their ostensible purpose—included opportunities for validation of claims to prestige through ostentatious allocation of gifts and demonstration of family privileges in the form of the family's own dances, songs, masks, rattles, and "privileged exhibitions." Furthermore, the individual himself, when he danced his own dance, clothed in his own costume symbolic of his "song," had opportunity for solo performance and display. All the old functions survive today. The winter dances are still called for a variety of purposes, and as in the past there is still opportunity for display of family and individual privileges. As several informants reported, most of the members of the Camas Band own either the "rattle" or the "mask" privileges, and pass these rights of display down to their children. "We're mostly rattlers around here," one resident of Village I explained, and when I asked if the rattles were still used much today, "Oh yes," he answered, "at the winter dances, to escort the dancers in. They used to be made of two big shells fastened together and filled with pebbles. When they got copper, they used this instead." Owners of the famous "swaihwe" masks are very few today, but are still occasionally hired to perform their dances in their full white swansdown regalia.

At all these dances or ceremonies, whether they are small local affairs or large ones to which a neighboring band may be invited, the gift giving is of lavish proportions, as we have already seen. Not only do all guests receive some such token as money or sugar to take away with them, but the sponsoring family may give special gifts to chosen relatives or friends. Mr. Wilson's daughter described this procedure, as it was carried out in connection with her naming ceremony: "My brother and I had to sit on a pile of blankets, and I had two around my shoulders, and a special band around my head. At the end, these blankets were given away to some relatives and friends. They were Hudson's Bay, and cost about fifty-four dollars. Some people today are using woolen sheets." Queried as to who the people were who had received the blankets, and why they had received them, and if this had been planned beforehand, the informant claimed that nothing had been planned. The blankets were simply given "to friends we like, and it was just decided when we saw them sitting there."

This suggests strongly the old system of reciprocal obligations and "gift giving" that actually masked a system of debts and loans. Though my queries did not uncover acknowledgments of any such motivation today, it does not seem unlikely that vestiges of the old system may still be operating. Even the superintendent suggested that something in the nature of the old exchanges may be going on beneath the surface, unknown to him. The only explanations I received from Indians relating the present system to the past came from one man who used the expression "return a favor" when he told of the reasons for gift giving, and from another who said, "The trouble with the dances is that they cost a lot to give. But the money does circulate. When we go up to the dances at N——, we get fifty cents, I, my wife, and so forth, so the money comes back to you. That's the Indian way." Whatever the underlying dynamics may be today, it is obvious that the status mechanism of gift giving is very much alive, as a value and as an actuality, the poverty of the Camas Indians notwithstanding. The Indian manages because he can count on the cooperation of a large kin group. Indeed, the cementing of kinship ties—both local and larger than local—in itself may constitute one of the important functions of the dances.

The individual can still lay claim to uniqueness and importance at the winter dances, not only through display of generosity, but through dance performance. There is some evidence that dancers build up reputations as "good" dancers, and "worth seeing," just as entertainers in White society do. An official in the Indian Office reported hearing such comments as "Beatrice danced last night, but she wasn't very good. Now Freddy is a good dancer. I'll go to see him." Entertainment, of course, was always one of the functions of the winter dances, during the slack winter season. Entertainment they still are today, drawing in even some of the White people of the town as occasional appreciative spectators—a factor of no little importance, probably, in enhancing the participating Indian's feeling of prestige as an Indian engaged in his traditional activities.

Though gift giving and display of family and individual prerogatives and names still constitute the social system underlying the winter dances, there are other functions of the dances, as in the past. The belief in spirit power and its lassitude and ailing that can be cured only through the dance initiation is still current. From numerous sources, Indian and White, accounts were given to me of young people restored to health through dancing, when doctors had despaired of helping them. One such report from the Indian Health Services nurse herself concerned a young tubercular girl with whom the doctor had been making no progress. "The Indians took her on a stretcher to the dances, and made her dance. Today she is a case of arrested TB, and mother of several children."

A local storekeeper told of the practice as she had seen it.

The dancers have to go through awful things even now when they are initiated. The Indians still take them up to a lake and make them bathe, even at that cold time of year, and they have to fast. When they come in to the dances they're so weak someone has to hold them up. But for some reason it does not seem to do them good. I knew of one girl who had been a puny, sickly creature, but after she was a dancer she was different. She really looked healthy and well.

Belief in the spirit power activating the dancer was attested to by an Indian father of fifty-nine years, who told of allowing one of his daughters who was subject to convulsions to be taken as a dancer.

> The Indian people said to me, "You'd better send her to the dances." I didn't want to, but there wasn't anything else to do, so she became a dancer, and is much better now. The dancers have the power, and this is what makes them dance. They're not just hopping up and down and dancing and whooping for fun. Even a young person like my girl, who doesn't know anything about the dances, doesn't hesitate when she's got the power. It's this power makes them dance.

It has been suggested in Barbara Lane's study of this Indian group, that in recent times there has been induction into the dances of young persons who did not show the traditional signs of spirit power. "A few accounts indicate that at least in post-contact times, induction of persons without power was consciously undertaken. These accounts involved young people who drank excessively or remained away from the reserve for long periods. Their induction, with consequent restrictions for the duration of the ceremonial season curtailed the undesirable behavior, at least for a time." [3] There is some evidence in statements of my informants that the use of dance initiation for this kind of control does, indeed, occur sometimes today. I was told in the Indian Office that the old people look around not only for sickly young people to initiate, but for those who have been drinking a lot and "running around," believing that dancing is a "cure" for this behavior. The case has already been mentioned of the young man whose mother forced him to become a dancer in hopes of getting him away from a girl who seemed to her undesirable as a daughter-in-law.

The whole complex of the winter dance ceremonies today, then, represents not only a survival of elements of a traditional system of relationships, status mechanisms, and religious belief, but contains features that are adaptable to modern problems

---

3. Barbara Lane, "A Comparative and Analytic Study of Some Aspects of Northwest Coast Religion" (Ph.D. diss., University of Washington, Seattle, 1953), p. 32.

and are aimed at exerting some social control over them. At the same time the dances offer the Indian an arena where he may keep alive his kinship ties and reaffirm his respect for tradition and his pride in being an Indian.

Some of the same points could be made concerning the Shaker practices which, though a phenomenon of post-contact times, offer the Indian the means of participating in social forms compatible with a number of his old practices and beliefs. He can achieve certain prestige satisfactions related at the same time to the old system and to a new one, and to the new problems of life as an Indian in the twentieth century.

Shakerism

The history of the Shaker movement since its inception in 1881, the premises upon which it is built, and its probable psychological significance for its members have been fully explored by Gunther,[4] Barnett,[5] Collins,[6] Voget,[7] and others. Its relationship to both Christian church practices and to Indian spirit dancing has been frequently pointed out, as well as its relationship to other "nativistic movements" such as the Ghost Dance and the Peyote cult. In his *Innovation: The Basis of Cultural Change,* Barnett has mentioned among the various appeals of Shakerism for its adherents its "permissiveness," that is, the wide scope offered for *individual* inspiration and expression; and its opportunities for travel from reserve to reserve for participation

---

4. Erna Gunther, "The Shaker Religion of the Northwest," in *Indians of the Urban Northwest,* Marian Smith, ed. (New York: Columbia University Press), 1949, pp. 37–76.

5. Homer G. Barnett, *Indian Shakers: A Messianic Cult of the Pacific Northwest* (Carbondale: Southern Illinois University Press, 1957).

6. June McCormick Collins, "The Indian Shaker Church: A Study of Continuity and Change in Religion," *Southwestern Journal of Anthropology* 6 (Winter 1950): 399–411.

7. Fred W. Voget, "The American Indian in Transition: Reformation and Accommodation," *American Anthropologist* 58 (April 1956): 249–63; idem, "The American Indian in Transition: Reformation and Status Innovations," *American Journal of Sociology* 62 (January 1957): 369–82.

in services, conventions, or reunions.[8] Voget has stressed the function of the religion as an effort to "reorganize and reform the Indian way," as the individual Indian "forms and reorganizes his self to attain public recognition." At the basis, he says, is the anxious concern of the Indian for ego-fulfillment and for brightening the self-image. Shakerism helps him achieve this through introducing a new set of statuses, including the claim he can lay to public recognition "provided he can furnish prima facie evidence of a transcendent and purifying experience in which God's blessing has conveyed power and transformed body and character."[9]

The possible array of meanings of the religion to the Camas participants cannot be explored to any great depth through observation and interview. But statements of the members, plus the evidence offered by observation of the service itself, can provide important clues.

Among the Camas constituents are some of the most prominent members of the band; one of them was elected chief in 1957; another has held the unpaid position of Indian constable since 1938 and is spoken of with respect by other Indians. Both men have had the honor of being written up in the local town newspaper as the featured local "citizen," in a series of articles devoted to prominent men of the district, both White and Indian. It was clear from the statements of both men that the Shaker influence on drinking habits was one of the paramount considerations in their minds. To quote from the newspaper article on the constable:

> A——'s father . . . was a man of some note. He was among those Indians who first brought the Shaker Church to the district. He helped build the first church in 1906 and later became its first bishop. Religion was something young A—— didn't treat too seriously at first. "I was crazy in those days," he said. "I was a drinking man and it wasn't so good. My children cried, there was no money and not enough to eat, I spent it all on liquor." When A——

---

8. Homer G. Barnett, *Innovation: The Basis of Cultural Change* (New York: McGraw-Hill Book Company, 1953).

9. Voget, "Reformation and Status Innovations," pp. 369–72.

quit drinking in 1938 all his family embraced the Shaker religion with him.

The chief of the band in 1957, when he talked about the religion with me, also emphasized the importance of the Shaker influence on drinking habits. He said that in his younger days he "went wrong" and was a bad drinker. Then he became a Shaker and has not touched liquor in eighteen years. He spoke fervently, yet with dignity, of what the Shaker religion means to him, how some of its songs have "touched" him, and of what good the religion can do. He brought up the case of a talented young Indian on the reserve who "makes a fool of himself drinking. He needs this kind of help so badly, but he can't be saved from his drinking habits because he's a very strong Catholic." The chief also stressed the importance of the religion's power to heal the sick, and described in vivid pantomime how he had once seen an old bedridden, paralyzed man rise up and move as some of the Shakers danced around him.

A third informant—Jack Harry, the spirit dancer and tradition-minded Indian, who is also a Shaker and a teetotaler—likewise stressed the importance of the religion's healing powers: "I've seen them cure a man whose legs were curled up to his chest, and his arms bent up like this. . . . They sang and prayed and his legs just began to come down and he was walking around, till someone made the mistake of touching him. It works for those who have faith; it's like that in any denomination." This statement, relating the healing to "faith" as in any denomination, might seem to suggest that for Mr. Harry the concept was not present of a Shaker "spirit of God," allied to the old guardian spirit concept, and bestowing "power." [10] It is likely, however, that if Mr. Harry had gone on to expand upon his beliefs, he would have sounded more like an Indian spirit dancer speaking. As it was, he was indeed stating one of the basic tenets of Shaker belief, that all the miracles flow from faith in God's power.

The chief's description of the cures seemed to relate the

10. See Collins, "Shaker Church," 403–4.

process somewhat more closely to the Indian belief in "power," though by no means did he equate the two. After explaining that a Shaker "finds" a song—that is, it "comes" to him—and that others learn his song and help him sing it, he explained that the ill person "catches the spirit of those that are present." Not only is there dancing and singing around him, but "we brush the ill person off. Our hands shake when we have the power, you know."

In the service observed by me in the small Shaker church in Village I, there was ample evidence of the shaking hands, fingers, arms, in every member of the congregation, and of "brushing off" of one another, with various motions of the vibrating arms, while the whole meeting was dominated by the rhythmic pulse of dancing feet, the loud rhythmic ringing of bells, and chanting voices. According to Lemert,[11] the brushing off is a technique for removing offensive spirits from a person. Barnett's explanation is that "sin" or "evil force" is counteracted in this way.[12]

Before describing more fully the nature of this service, some of its Christian elements might be pointed out. The church itself resembles other Christian churches, except that the belfry is at the far end and not at the entrance; the long axis of the church is oriented in an east-west direction, according to Shaker specifications. Inside, there is an altar, or "prayer table," at the front, upon which stand crosses and candles and religious pictures, as well as the large shiny bells used in the service. The dominating element in the room is a large wooden construction in the shape of a cross, disposed in a fashion peculiar to the Shaker church. Suspended from the ceiling, it lies horizontally above the heads of the dancing congregation, and is beautifully and spectacularly lighted by the upright candles outlining its shape. The crosses on the prayer table serve as candleholders, as well.

---

11. Edwin M. Lemert, *Alcohol and the Northwest Coast Indians*, University of California Publications in Culture and Society, vol. 2, no. 6 (Berkeley and Los Angeles: University of California Press, 1954), p. 367.
12. Barnett, *Innovation*, p. 150.

The atmosphere in the church is dignified and quiet, before the service begins. People enter, talking in whispers, and then disperse, the men going to the men's side and the women to the women's as in the local Catholic church for Indians. However, here in the Shaker church there are no pews. The men and women simply go to long benches against the walls, on their respective sides of the room. A row of benches near the entrance accommodates children, who do not participate.

On the summer Saturday night of my attendance with two White friends, it was about 10:00 P.M. before the service began. There were no lights whatever outside the church, or along the road leading to the church from the highway. This was in accord with Shaker belief that only candlelight is holy, and no electric or gas lights must profane the scene. We shuffled and stumbled along hunting for the path to the entrance. Soon a few other people appeared from the darkness ahead of us and walked into the church one by one. They must have been standing out there, a little beyond the church, waiting. No one spoke.

Inside, about fifteen men and fifteen women assembled, ranging in age from the twenties to the eighties—a small group, we were told, because it was summertime and many were away. Some ten young children occupied the benches near the entrance. A number of the congregation were Indians who had come up from a reserve near Victoria. A gray-haired old man walked over to us as we entered, and extended his hand. "Welcome to our church. I trust you are believers in God?" Receiving affirmative answers he shook our hands. "The spirit of God is here," he went on to explain. "We have come here to do our work and heal the sick. Each one sings his own song. That's what we believe in, and we believe the spirit of God is here with us." After shaking our hands warmly again, he went back to the men's bench.

The first part of the service included a number of Christian elements. A leader spoke briefly to the standing congregation, in Indian. Several members made the sign of the cross; at least one knelt for a while, facing the altar; a collection was taken, or perhaps one should say, received. Individuals walked up one by one, men first, women later, and dropped their coins noisily into a plate on the altar. But even this early part of the service included a dance-like march in circular formation around the room; the stamping of feet marked the rhythm and two or three men added to the accent with the shaking of the large bells, while everyone sang together a simple chanted phrase. Early in the service, too, there were evidences of vibrations in the arms, hands, and fingers of several of the congregation, as well as of shaking and clapping the hands in motions of brushing off the legs and thighs.

After the collection, the healing of the sick began, with all members participating in dancing, chanting, vibrating, in unison, yet each with his own style of stepping and vibrating within the unbroken, overall rhythm. Three who sought healing sat in straight wooden chairs placed in a row across the church, facing the altar. The three were a stout middle-aged woman, a baby held by a grandmother, and a very wizened little old lady. One man, who seemed to take the lead in all of the healing efforts, rolled up his sleeves and stepped forward with a candle in his hands. He stood before each one of the three ill persons in turn, making the healing gesture of flicking something on them from the candle flame, four times from the front, four times from the rear. Then he began a quiet laying on of hands, beginning with the middle-aged woman, and the rest of the congregation converged around her also, dancing and singing, while three or four of them rang the large bells as they danced. The remaining hour of the service which we witnessed was devoted to this unbroken dancing and chanting, with concentration around the three ailing persons, yet also with individuals taking the opportunity to approach each other with vibrating hands and arms outstretched.

One man, for instance, approached a woman who was seated on the women's side, and let his arm and vibrating fingers shake over her for a moment or two. A young woman, with her hair in two braids hanging down to her shoulders, began moving around the room in a trance-like step. She stopped in front of a young man and began to make motions of cupping something off his neck and chest and throwing it away. Also, she took his hands and swung his arms in a rhythmic movement with hers, and rubbed his chest and shoulders lightly, making motions of transferring something from herself to him, no doubt attempting to transmit her power. The young man's face, throughout all this, held an expression of intense concentration.

I have called the rhythm and the chanting "unbroken," but this is not quite accurate. Every ten or fifteen minutes there were small but perceptible shifts in both the phrase of syllables that was chanted, and the pace of the rhythm, as one individual after another took the lead to introduce his song and rhythm, and all the others joined in to "help" him.

There was great variety, also, in the way individuals stepped to the rhythm, and in the ways they adapted to the general rhythm of the group. One man who had begun very quietly increased his speed and movement until his action looked like a vigorous pantomime of a figure climbing a ladder, while standing in place. Some dancers stepped very lightly; one man pounded the floor so heavily that it seemed as though he might break it in. The floor was, as a matter of fact, heaving up and down, and the benches at the walls vibrating rhythmically. The room was filled with deafening noise and hypnotic rhythm. However, the demeanor of all the participants was not the least frenzied or convulsive. The facial expressions were intent and concentrated; the dancing steps, though often done heavily, did not involve uncontrolled throwing around of the body. Dignity characterized the entire scene.

It is impossible to say what various meanings participation in this service may have had for the array of individuals present. It is obvious, however, that at least part of what was being performed bore a close relationship to old Indian religious and social traditions; hardly surprising, seeing that among the Camas, initiated spirit dancers can and do belong to the Shaker faith. The service provides evidence that it offers wide scope for the individualism of the Indian, as the winter spirit dances do. As a Shaker, the Indian has the opportunity to contact and use a supernatural force called "power," without the intermediary of a priest; he can take individual leadership in introducing the phrase and beat which are his own, for others to pick up and follow. Even the ostentatious manner of offering money for the collection may bear some relationship to the Indian's traditional way of handling debts and pride through a mechanism of public display. Furthermore, as Voget has also noted, the personal relationships of the service stress social equality and personal worth, always a strong theme in the old Indian social system. There is no hierarchical structure of authority operating. The leader's part in the service is very minimal.[13]

It is not difficult to see how the Camas individual who has not broken completely with the traditional Indian dancing and singing ways can find in Shakerism sources of prestige satisfaction for himself in the old Indian terms. Furthermore, the control that Shakerism helps him gain over his problems of drinking, as well as the aid that he feels he is extending to others who are ailing or going to pieces, may well be a major source of prestige, and one that does indeed help him attain a brightening of his self-image as he looks at himself in relationship not to other Indians on the reserve, but to the White people with whom he lives and works in such close contact. This is all the more probable since at least some of the important townspeople—as evidenced by the tone of the newspaper article quoted—look upon and speak of the Shaker religion with respect.

Drinking

A discussion of the drinking behavior of the Camas Indian is pertinent at this point, since it seems evident that some of the drinking patterns, even though a phenomenon of post-contact times, embody features from the old traditional system of interpersonal relationships and ways of reckoning status. Of course, drinking and intoxication among the Indians today undoubtedly fulfill many diverse and complex functions, which only an exhaustive study and analysis, comparable to that of Lemert,[14] could explore. Our evidence here must be confined largely to that which observation in the beer parlor, and other overt acts, provides.

13. Voget, "Reformation and Status Innovations," 372.
14. Lemert, *Alcohol.*

The beer parlor behavior of the Camas Indian, as mentioned before, is not rowdy or violent. The trouble—fighting of Indian with Indian—usually begins out on the street afterwards. Inside the beer parlor there is quiet sitting with wife or friends, or conviviality with a larger group. On one of the nights of my observation, the room was noisy with voices and clatter, in an atmosphere which seemed prevailingly friendly. There was no segregation of Indians and non-Indians at tables in separate sections of the room. Indians moved about from table to table, greeting their friends. A young man in his twenties, whose home —actually his father's home—I had visited briefly on a previous occasion, came over to the table where I was sitting with friends, shook our hands, and sat down with us, in a most loquacious and friendly frame of mind. All were dressed neatly, the younger people as well as some of the middle-aged in summer sports clothes. Waiters kept the tables filled with new bottles. This was early on a Friday evening. The beer parlor, of course, is patronized day and night by the habitual drinkers. Large amounts of beer are consumed and a great deal of money is spent. The heavy drinkers become intoxicated eventually and end in violent behavior on the streets and in drunken driving.

One cannot escape the conclusion that the beer parlor offers an arena for the social interchange that has always been a valued part of Camas life; it offers, also, opportunities for display of hospitality and lavish spending—to say nothing of opportunity to exercise some of the old rivalry patterns. As one of the workers in the Indian Office explained, "The way the Indians treat someone they don't like is to send a whole case of beer over to his seat at the beer parlor. Then he has to reciprocate with even more."

Lemert suggests, also, that through the display of drinking large amounts, the individual Indian is finding a way of maximizing and maintaining his status in the eyes of others. To quote Lemert, whose study includes Indians of the Camas region, "From their mien and manner in pouring and downing large glasses of wine, beer, or whisky, many natives seem to be saying,

'Look, this is the way I drink.' "[15] It will be remembered that status, in Camas terms, has always involved individual display, to validate the right to prestige. An additional appeal of the beer parlor, of course, may lie in the right extended to the Indian to enjoy it on equal terms with the White man.

Beer parlor drinking to excess, however, is only one facet of the liquor problem. The illegal sale of whisky and other liquors to Indians, intoxication, and accompanying violence, have been problems since the White man brought liquor into the Indians' lives, and there is no sign of decrease. We can only summarize here what seem to be some of the most pertinent suggestions made by Lemert and others relative to the appeal of intoxication per se to the Indians.

There is, of course, the obvious appeal of escape from frustrations. Hawthorn, Belshaw, and Jamieson suggest:

Little prestige is associated with "holding liquor"; more is associated with getting drunk. This of course does not apply to all Indian drinkers, but it is true of a substantial proportion. For many of them, driven by the personal and social tensions of their confused life, intoxication is a blessed escape; a release from thought and responsibility for a few hours; a state which turns tiredness and despondency into well being or aggressive energy.[16]

Others have likened the appeal of intoxication to the appeal of the "ecstatic state" always valued by the Indians, and induced in the dance initiation rites. Lemert quotes a Swinomish Indian: "You get crazy when you sing. You don't want to eat anything, just drink water. You get crazy just like when you drink liquor."[17]

Lemert suggests also that the Indian values intoxication as an act of aggression against the White man, who has imputed infer-

15. Ibid., p. 324.
16. H. B. Hawthorn, C. S. Belshaw, and S. M. Jamieson, *The Indians of British Columbia: A Study of Contemporary Social Adjustment* (Berkeley and Los Angeles: University of California Press, 1958), pp. 379–80.
17. Lemert, *Alcohol*, p. 352.

iority to him in forbidding him free access to liquor.[18] And Hawthorn, Belshaw, and Jamieson make a pertinent suggestion relative to the crimes of personal violence so often accompanying the intoxication, and so much more frequently committed against other Indians than directed at White individuals:

> We can conjecture that the tensions inherent in the position of the Indian group and the maintenance of social distance find a kind of "permissible" expression in violence towards other Indians, but cannot find similarly acceptable expressions aimed overtly at the dominant group. Certainly, our data seem to reflect a tacit approval by White authority of Indian aggression towards Indians, a tolerance which would not extend to Indian acts of aggression aimed at Whites.[19]

Such interpretations as the above, and many offered in Lemert's study, bring us to the threshold of psychological investigation. We can only suggest here that those leads which recognize the status problems of the Indian, as well as those which relate his present values and social habits to those of his immediate past, would seem to us among the most important to explore, for further understanding of the liquor problem.

My own data suggest one pertinent conclusion which should not be overlooked: the Indian's drinking problem is not entirely a matter of "attraction" to the beer parlor or to the intoxicated state, or to the aggression against the Whites which intoxication may symbolize. It is partly a matter of lack of means of control over excessive drinking. Certainly the statements of many of my Indian informants—some of them already quoted in the section on Shakerism—indicated that at least some of the Indians themselves have sensed the ruin inherent in the situation, and have been seeking ways of controlling their own behavior. It must be remembered that in the traditional culture there was no alcohol and no intoxication to be dealt with. The Indian has entered the White man's world with the liquor bottle

18. Ibid., p. 336.
19. Hawthorn, Belshaw, and Jamieson, *Social Adjustment*, p. 327.

thrust into his hands, and no system of social control built in behind him to cope with the problem. The old family "headman" is almost extinct, and his was a limited authority anyway. Catholicism, it is evident, has not offered ways and means of control that have reached all who are nominally Catholics. Is this because a belief in personal sin and a punishing Deity has been foreign to the Camas' own system of religious belief?

Lastly, it must be pointed out that the Canadian law in itself has failed to offer effective controls. One cogent quotation from Hawthorn, Belshaw, and Jamieson will indicate the nature of some of the failure:

> Drinking parties in beer parlours are sometimes lively, noisy and good humoured and, very seldom, violent. Drinking parties outside beer parlours fall into two broad classes—those modelled on White behavior, and those where liquor is used as an adjunct of some traditional purpose. Naturally, the White behaviour that serves as a model is that which is most obviously there to be copied; and this, almost by definition, is the noisiest and most dramatic and exciting. It consists of rowdy drinking near dance halls, beer drinking in cars, and promiscuous parties. The other patterns of White drinking—the occasional glass of beer with a meal at home, or the social occasion where the guests take liquor as a refreshment—are observed by a very small minority of Indians, and, even if they wish to copy them, they cannot afford to do so. For paradoxically, the wild and secretive drinking is safer, because precautions are taken, and there is a certain anonymity in a crowd. Moderate drinking at home is not only illegal, but in this context it appears senseless—the danger of arrest increases as the time draws out, the possibility of informing increases because acquaintances are excluded, and anxiety over possible interruption and arrest is felt more keenly because the drinkers are more sober—and who would risk arrest anyway for just one or two glasses of beer? Once again, the law has contributed directly to immoderate drinking.[20]

In this section, as well as in those immediately preceding, I have attempted to point out that much of the present can be understood by reference to the social system of the past: its status mechanisms, its social and economic organization, the

20. Ibid., pp. 380-81.

customs binding the family and group life—in short, "the framework of relationships upon which custom moves," to use a particularly descriptive phrase from Arensberg and Kimball.[21] Today the old tools are being applied to the new problems. Indeed, a full set of new tools is not yet available to the Indian.

Perhaps it should be further stressed here, before we move on to consider the lives of the younger generations, that within this framework of relationships, the Camas Indian today presents the appearance of strong "individualism" as in the past. I have referred to this individualism in connection with the persistence of the winter ceremonies, the appeal of the Shaker religion, the difficulty the Indian often experiences in adapting to work under supervision. It should be added that in his mien and manner he shows his personal pride. The Camas Indian of 1954 has not become an apathetic, submissive individual, in the front he shows to the world. He does not accept his poverty, his uncertainties about land boundaries, and his history of transactions with the White man, without complaint.

In my conversations with Indians, after the firm handclasp and the forthright introduction, "I am Mr. ———," came the punctuations of complaint:

   The Indians get arrested for fishing in their *own* river.
   The Indians were never recompensed for the land taken from them. This reserve used to be 14,550 acres. Now it's only 8,500.

Furthermore, the Indian smilingly describes not only his children as "stubborn," but himself as "independent." His individualism is a part of his self-image:

   The Indian is very independent. He doesn't always want to stay on a job.
   My son didn't get along in the school here very well. He was kind of independent. So then he went to the residential school, but he didn't like it. I never liked school either.

21. Conrad M. Arensberg and Solon T. Kimball, *Family and Community in Ireland* (Cambridge: Harvard University Press, 1940), p. 311.

The Indian's personal expressiveness—his "solo performance" entered into for the purpose of attaining well-being—continues and reaches beyond his public behavior in ceremonies, extending even into his life at home. The Indian is a singer, and he composes songs for himself about his private bereavements and sorrows, to relieve his feelings. These songs are "his," as are the spirit songs.

"This is a song I stole from my sister," an Indian explained to me, as he told how he had helped collect and translate songs to be used in a musical production based on Indian life—a production managed by a capable teacher in the Indian day school and performed for White audiences. "It's her song about feeling lonely when her parents died." Another was a neighbor's song of weeping for the dead; another, his own brother's song about how sad he had felt when he was in the army, away from his songs. None of these songs, of course, was a private "power" song of the kind sung at dances.

It is important to keep in mind the possibility that this expressive channel, as well as other aspects of the Indian's individualism, need not be lost, as the old ways gradually take new shape.

YOUNG PEOPLE: OLD WAY OR NEW?

The ways of the past are discernible in many respects in the lives of the young people today. Until recently uneducated and unequipped for a range of vocations, young Camas men and women have not been able to strike out on their own. Instead, they marry young, as was the custom of their forebears, and settle down in a corner of the paternal home, staying there perhaps five or six years until separate housing is made available.

Though education up to age sixteen became compulsory twenty years ago, until recently it was more of a goal than a fact, and even now the sixteenth birthday finds a number of young people just finishing the eighth grade, and by no means half way through high school. For instance, of the six students graduating from the eighth grade of the Indian day school in 1953, one was fourteen, three were fifteen, two sixteen. The

1956 graduates included two who were fourteen, and four fifteen-year-olds. This situation is understandable at least partly in terms of the difficulties besetting Indian children from the very day of school entrance. In many cases, introduction to school has meant largely introduction to the English language, as well as to conventions concerning dress and cleanliness. Absenteeism, too, has been a major problem. Children have missed school not only because of the winter dances but because of simple poverty. As the superintendent said, "Sometimes families get so hard up that they just take the children out of school and go off clam-digging."

High school has probably held few allurements for the average Indian boy in the immediate past. The only jobs he thinks of as potentially open to him—the logging and longshoring jobs of his fathers—do not require education; and he can enter the labor force at sixteen if he wants to. As far as high school education for girls is concerned, parents commonly express no desire to have their daughters undertake it. "What use is it? Look at the Gordon girls. They graduated from high school but couldn't get jobs."

The Camas girl of sixteen is thinking of marriage, as her mother and grandmother did before her. The young Camas man, too, begins early to look for a mate in his own or a nearby band. He does not go off alone to the States to seek his fortune, leaving his family and the reserve and its security behind him. When she marries, the Camas girl today is generally about eighteen and a half, and the young man about twenty and a half, as indicated by study of data from Village I and Village II.[22]

---

22. *Village I.* Of the eighteen young women of thirty or younger who were or had been "married," age of marriage could be ascertained for sixteen, showing a range from fourteen and a half to twenty-four years of age, with the median at eighteen and a half. Of the fourteen young married men, age of marriage could be figured for twelve, showing a range from fourteen and a half to twenty-eight years of age, with the median at twenty and a half.

Village II. Figures are less meaningful than for Village I, because of lack of first-hand knowledge, especially in the cases of men shown on the lists as unmarried. However, the sixteen young women under thirty listed as mar-

As already pointed out, spinsters and bachelors are extremely rare in Camas society. The young people are fairly certainly headed toward marriage. There were only ten unmarried girls in Village I, of sixteen or over, in 1954. The oldest of these was twenty-two and a half, the median falling between eighteen and eighteen and a half. The oldest of the nineteen Village I men over sixteen listed as unmarried was forty-seven, but I have already mentioned that there is some doubt that he was actually single, though shown so in the band list. The median age of the unmarried men was twenty.

A great many marriages take place between members of the various villages within the Camas Band, and even between members of the same village. Owing to lack of data, it is not possible to make comparisons with the situation that existed before the entry of the White man, but it seems more than likely that a change has come about. In the old days it was considered advisable to seek hospitality through marriages contracted with members of families outside of the immediate locale. As this necessity has disappeared and free choice of mates by the young people themselves has become a more common practice, less attention is probably paid to residence of the prospective mate. Distance of relationship, however, is still important, and marriages with first cousins are avoided.

Study of the complete register of the band reveals that fifty (or forty-one percent) of the marriages of young people during the recent ten-year period of 1943 to 1953 have been between members of the band. In seventy-one marriages (or fifty-nine percent) one partner belonged either to a different band or was non-Indian. However, in approximately half of these seventy-one cases the "different band" was one of twelve nearby small

---

ried ranged in age from thirteen to twenty-two years of age at time of marriage, with the median at eighteen and a half. The eleven young men listed as married or known to have common-law wives ranged from seventeen and a half to twenty-three years of age at time of marriage, with the median falling between twenty and twenty and a half.

When the union is a common-law one, I have figured "age of marriage" as one year prior to birthdate of the first infant.

bands closely related to the Camas in language and customs and administered by the same agency.[23]

The records show that since 1931 thirty women have married "non-Indians" (mainly Whites, Filipinos, Mexicans, or American Indians). Five additional women at one time married non-Indians but are currently back on either the Camas or a nearby reserve. Many of these marriages to non-Indians occurred during the war years or shortly thereafter, from 1943 to 1949. There has been none recorded between 1950 and 1954. The war-time boom may indicate that when the opportunity presents itself, the Indian girl is quite capable of leaving her band and her Indian birthright and privileges, to marry whom she pleases.

Since the majority of the young people marry Indians nearby and stay fairly close to home, the result is that the band remains an entity and retains its numbers. It does not, however, retain a complete unity or harmony between the generations. As the young people settle down in the paternal home, there are sources of conflict today that did not exist in the past. There is a new way of life that can be chosen, and those who choose it must inevitably assert themselves against the old way of the grandparents. We have seen one instance of this in the case of the eighteen-year-old Paul Harry daughter, who was at odds with her parents over the matter of a legal marriage ceremony.

Other conflicts, as we have already mentioned, arise over choice of mate. The young people are encouraged by the priest and by new custom to make free choices. The parents and grandparents, however, knowing that the young couple will live in their home and become inevitably involved in its economic

---

23. In arriving at these figures, marriages were included which took place between 1943 and 1953, with a few in 1954 which had been entered in the Village I list. Those common-law unions which produced children were considered marriages. Young people who were age thirty or younger at time of marriage were included in this count. In a few cases, one partner to the marriage was known to be over thirty. Some ages of non-Indian husbands were not entered in the list. It seems safe to assume that the majority were young men. It is unusual for Camas girls to marry men who are more than two or three years older than themselves.

arrangements, feel and act as they did in the past under these circumstances. They attempt to direct choice of mate and even begin financial transactions. Sometimes the young people defer to the parents' wishes; sometimes they run to the priest for refuge.

In other ways, too, the young people may try to assert themselves against their elders, as they could not when chaperonage was stricter and authority clearly in the hands of the headman of the household. We have seen how Margaret Gordon struggled to discipline her daughter Elsie to keep her from going into beer parlors and running off alone to the States and generally "going crazy," as the Indians say.

That some of the young people themselves feel the need for stronger controls was suggested by one mother who was having difficulties disciplining her teen-age daughter and was welcoming the help of the Kamloops boarding school in this regard. The mother claimed that the daughter likewise appreciated the confining environment of the school. "If she stayed here she'd just be wanting to run out to the movies all the time, and I couldn't keep her home. She's such a jolly girl, it's hard for her to stay home. And she's anxious to pass her school work. She wants to get trained for nurse's work. She thinks she studies better at Kamloops."

The Catholic church a few years ago attempted to organize a club for young people, but has given up—at least temporarily—in the face of the young folks' desire to make the club meet their recreational needs in their own terms. The priest said: "I wanted the boys and girls to learn how to have good times together, for educational and religious purposes. But it developed that they didn't want to do anything but dance, so I'm sort of letting the club drop. I think after a while they'll come around of their own accord and want more of what the club started out to be."

The winter dances are another potential source of conflict for young people today. Those who are looking toward the new way of life fear the possibility of being "seized" and initiated, for a number of reasons. To some, the whole winter dance complex seems "crazy." And those who want to try to hold steady jobs know, as one man said, that "if you become a dancer, you're no good for anything from December to March." Yet at the same time the dances are entertainment, and they exert an appeal for this reason if for no other, as the trips to the berry fields do also. What else is there for recreation and excitement on the reserve or in the town? There are a few small cafes where one can sit and drink pop; there is a skating arena where occasional wrestling matches and dances are held; and there is the town's one movie. Only a handful of young men play on the town's mixed teams or on teams in Victoria. The all-Indian soccer team, organized by the Catholic church, fell apart when the beer parlor opened its doors to the Indians. The beer parlor attracts the young men as well as the old, and in itself becomes a potential source of conflict, as we know from our observation that a number of young people are seeking the controls over drinking that Shakerism seems to promise.

There is even conflict between the young people themselves, as some choose education and the new way of life, and others gang up against those who make these choices. We have mentioned already the boy and girl gangs, especially the Black Hawks, composed at least partly of the uneducated "flats" boys. This gang behavior is perhaps the counterpart, in adolescent terms, of the way some adult Indians feel and behave toward the Mr. Wilsons who are moving successfully toward the White man's way. There is the possibility also, as suggested by Hawthorn, Belshaw, and Jamieson, that the young people's gangs have been formed in a spirit of rebellion against older Indians as well as against White contemporaries, because of a feeling of alienation from the ways of both of these groups and the need of the support of some kind of social grouping.[24]

The general impression of the Camas Reserve, however, is not of one torn by dissension. In 1954 many Indians knew nothing of the Black Hawk gang. In 1957 the gang was no longer even in existence, according to the informant who, in 1954, had provided the fullest details. Living next door to each other are

24. Hawthorn, Belshaw, and Jamieson, *Social Adjustment*, p. 336.

young people who go the old way—becoming dancers in the winter, working irregularly, spending months at a time in the States—and those who go the new way. "I try to do what I can for my children," said one of the latter, a young man of twenty-seven, who sat talking with me in his neat stucco home; "I've worked steadily in lumber for seven years."

Even the conflicts between the generations are probably of lesser proportions than could arise in those Indian communities where vocational opportunities for the young are markedly different than for the old, and require radical changes in dress, manners, habits, or speech, for successful participation. The young Camas Indian, working in the timber or on the docks, has had no need of skills or appearances that are different from his father's.

Life on the Camas Reserve holds together in spite of the pull of the new way against the old. The image comes to mind of batter on a griddle, bubbling at the edges and internally, but retaining its shape as it takes on a new texture. One of the forces making for this cohesion may well be the childhood experience of the members of the band. As we shall see in the next section, there is ample evidence of that indulgence of the small child which can develop in him "an affectionate loyalty to the parents." [25] And there is ample evidence of this loyalty, as married young people converge upon the parental home for Sunday dinner, bringing along all the grandchildren; as young wives make frequent visits to parents; and as parents drive long distances to see the married daughters. There is respect and affection, too, in the tones of voice, whenever references are made to "my late mother" and "my late dad."

THE CHILDREN AND THEIR CHALLENGE

The Camas infant today is born in the hospital in the town. Preparations have been made at home for his arrival. Clean baby clothes and blankets await him, and possibly a crib or carriage.

---

25. Gordon MacGregor, *Warriors Without Weapons: A Study of the Society and Personality Development of the Pine Ridge Sioux* (Chicago: University of Chicago Press, 1946), p. 56.

In some homes his bed will be a cradle suspended from the ceiling. The descendant of the aboriginal cradle board which hung from a cedar branch in the Big House, today's cradle is made of wood in the shape of a shallow box, or consists simply of a draped blanket attached to a hanging spring, and placed over or beside the parents' bed, within arm's reach.

The Indian Health Services nurse sees the mother and baby in her office in the town, if they will come, and makes visits to the homes to advise on baby care. The present nurse, who has been on the reserve for six years, has been introducing to Indian mothers the idea that babies need not wait until they are weaned to begin eating solid foods. "I have found Indian mothers aghast," she said, "at the idea that a baby should have solid food as young as three months. Their custom has been to give nothing but the bottle or the breast for a whole year and to nurse the baby whenever it cried." She reported also that during her six years of service she had seen an increasing use of the bottle. "Mothers used to nurse their babies more than they do now. The tendency now is to get the baby on the bottle so the parents can go off. They will leave milk in a thermos bottle for the rest of the children to give to the baby, and then go off to the beer parlor as early as 9:00 A.M."

My observations in the homes, and my queries of ten mothers, revealed that there is still nursing whenever the baby frets and that the nursing or bottle period comes to an end when the baby is between nine months and a year old. Invariably mothers indicated that weaning was a matter of the baby's stopping, as though of his own accord:

> I nurse my babies for about nine months. They just stop then and eat everything.
>
> My two-year-old was nursed for nine months and only took the bottle one month after that.
>
> I nursed him till he was about a year old, and then he just began to eat everything.

These comments suggest the assumption that the baby has a certain independence; that he will grow in his own way. Indeed, mothers were flexible about the weaning arrangements, and seemed to follow their infants' desires. Several mothers reported that their children of eighteen months or two years still took the bottle at times. As one said, "She wants it when she goes to sleep."

The same flexibility and lack of pressure were evidenced in the attitudes toward toilet training. In general, children were learning to keep dry at about eighteen months, but there was great variation, seeming to stem from a casual attitude on the part of the mothers, perhaps influenced by expediency. In one family, the second child had been trained early, at thirteen months, "because we were going berrying," but no such situation had prompted early training for the first child. The mother began her efforts with him when he was fifteen months old, and the training was accomplished by twenty-two months. Another mother explained that she had begun training early with her little girl, but had dropped her efforts in the face of practical difficulties. "It was hard because we don't have running water, just an outhouse way back there. So I gave up." A third mother spoke in a way that attributed to the child herself some of the credit for the accomplishment of training at one year. "She was real quick. My brother's girl is still wetting at two years."

Not all parents who were queried could report the ages at which their children had learned to walk. The attitude toward the attainment of this skill seemed to be one of taking it for granted.

As he becomes a toddler and enters the period of early childhood, the child's conflicts with his parents are mild and few. Neither frustrations nor consequent aggressions ruffle his life or that of the parents. All my White informants who had had close contact with Indian families stressed again and again that Indian parents seldom punished their children, seldom denied them anything. Though Camas parents themselves, as they talked with me, claimed that they did scold and "yell at" their children sometimes, my own observations led me to feel that discipline was extraordinarily mild and that the young child's manipulative and exploratory urges were given very free rein.

One reason for this may be that there is little in the average Indian house that needs protection. Rugs and breakable decorative objects are absent. An eighteen-month-old boy who takes a little key and wanders around his house trying to poke it into every available chink in floors or walls or furnishings is damaging nothing. But an additional factor seems to be that parents, as well as some grandparents, placidly accept the children's behavior. They are not easily annoyed. I have seen a grandmother make no move to restrain a child who was grabbing her skirt and tugging heavily, as we two adults conversed. I have seen a mother make no move to take from her three-year-old a family snapshot which the child was fingering very roughly. I have seen a grandfather, a carpenter by profession, allow his four-year-old grandson to walk around hammering nails into the living room walls and door frames of the newly-built house the family lived in.

At times this acceptance on the part of the adults appears to be due to a feeling of helplessness, or to capitulation as controlling authorities. But there may be other roots in temperament or tradition which cannot be fully explored here. One can, however, raise the questions: Is there a relation between the indulging, nonpunitive behavior of adults and the old belief that if a baby is not kept happy and protected from quarrels, he may choose to go back to babyland? Or with the old belief that children are without guardian spirits to protect and help them? Is there a relation between the readiness of parents today to allow independence in children and the old belief in early preparation for spirit-seeking?

The helplessness of many parents as controlling authorities is not a conjecture, but an easily observed fact, and may be explained at least partly in terms of the difficulties of taking on new roles in a time of transition. As I have pointed out before, it is only recently that young parents, moving into their own homes, have had to learn to rely upon themselves, rather than upon their own parents, for the training and disciplining of their children. Their ineffectiveness was evidenced to me again and again in such comments as the following:

> I can't get my children into bed until it's dark. I can't get them in to eat, either.
>
> Right now just about all my children eat is berries. They go down to the river first thing in the morning and don't come up until they get hungry.
>
> I don't do anything in the evening but go to bed. That's because I can't get my Alice to bed unless I go with her.

Occasionally during my visits to the homes, parents made mild remonstrances when the children became very noisy or interruptive. In one case, I felt that the mother's gentle reproof, spoken only once, indicated that she did not really assess the behavior as particularly objectionable. In another case, a mother did appear to want her child to stop his monopolizing of our attention, and made several softly-voiced suggestions such as, "Go play outdoors now," or "Don't do that, sweetie." The child did not go outdoors and never completely stopped his interrupting. His pattern of obeying his mother was to rein in his activities ever so slightly, when she spoke to him, so that she was temporarily mollified, and he could continue with what he wanted to do. The relationship between mother and child actually remained very pleasant throughout the hour-long visit. This was a mother who said to me once, when I asked her in private if she ever punished this little boy, "Oh no. If I punished him, I'd feel sick myself."

The preschool child, then—even one as young as two years old—lives a relatively unrestricted life. As a two-year-old, he may already have been shunted off the mother's lap, because a new baby may have come along and because there is no expectation on the parents' part that he needs his mother's constant care at this age. He joins the group of young children—boys and girls—who play around all day outside of the house or down by the river.

These young children explore and experiment. Though they have been provided with a few store toys, such as small plastic trucks and cars, water pistols, dolls, and coloring books, they play also with makeshift materials. I have seen children making slingshots, improvising a bow and arrow with two sticks, and using an old length of water pipe as a gun. A little boy of about six was seen imitating a winter dancer. For a costume he had draped a bandanna from his waist to his knees, and over his head he had thrown a woman's old fur piece. Children waiting outside of the beer parlor in a little park were seen inventing jumping games as they hobbled their legs with scarves.

As they wander about in their play, free of supervision, many children become dirty and neglected in appearance. It is only the most acculturated parents who make an effort to keep their young children clean throughout childhood as well as early infancy. Furthermore, the poor diet—which may be limited at times to berries, candy, and pop, if the children so choose—destroys the teeth and lowers resistance. The nurse reported that children particularly between the ages of two and five were apt to become ill enough to be taken to the hospital. Sores, pneumonia, and malnutrition were the common complaints.

These wandering, undernourished children should not be thought of, however, as unloved or unwanted at home. Quite the contrary, all my evidence points to affectionate, warm relationships between parents, or grandparents, and children. Fathers as well as mothers were gentle, playful, and demonstrative with their young ones. As I made my visits in the homes, conversations were generally carried on in the midst of numerous children. There appeared to me nothing unusual in the way a seven-year-old girl, in one home, stood beside her father's chair and once reached out and stroked his hair, as he and I talked.

Strikingly illustrative of the parental attitude toward children was an account the nurse gave of a father whose twelve-year-old son had had serious heart trouble. The father had spent hours at a time sitting with the boy on his lap, "holding on to his heart." Finally, after the doctors took the child to the hospital for treatment, he died. The father mourned, "It wouldn't have happened if I'd kept him with me." "He was probably right," the nurse said. "It was the feeling of human closeness, and the affectionate care and support of the father that nourished the boy and kept him alive."

Large families of children are wanted today as they were in the past, at least partly for the same reason. The economy of abundance in the old days, and the presence of many women in the Big House made it possible for families to welcome the arrival of children and to bring them up without hardship. Today, though the economy has changed, a basic security remains. Every parent knows that the government will not let Indian children go without food or clothing, and that it will supply medical care and education as well. And if a mother should find herself too burdened as her infants arrive in close succession, she knows that an aunt, a grandmother, or a sister can be found who will take one of the babies to rear. The assumption is that all people want to have children around. Indeed, the comments made to me by women who were bringing up or caring temporarily for children not their own all expressed this feeling. One woman said of the nephew she was rearing and the distantly related orphan she was keeping for the summer, "Oh, they're full of mischief. I sure have to keep talking to them, but it's nice having them around."

Not every Indian child has a nuclear family intact, but each one has a group of nurturing kinfolk, and each one lives in the band as well as in his own home. Within this large system of relationships he is cherished and cared for, and he is expected to have a share in the common experiences. Though he is kept away from funerals, as in the old days, he goes with his family to the winter dances, to the Shaker services, or to mass at the Catholic church. His annual summer trips to the States may begin when he is as young as a year old.

If he is one of the children selected for boarding school, this wrench from home may be difficult for him, but even this experience is within the Camas tradition. His parents or his aunts and uncles may very well have attended the same institution. All his life he has heard their tales of school. And when he himself leaves home, his cousins and his neighbors and sometimes his brothers leave with him.

When he begins his school life, the Camas child leaves behind him his period of unrestricted freedom and enters a world where he is presented with unfamiliar tasks. He must now speak English, and no matter what school he attends—public, boarding, or Catholic day school—he encounters the curriculum and texts that are standard for the Province and oriented toward Canadian life. In the Catholic schools there are catechism classes and religious services, in addition. For the children in the camp-like households it is not surprising that these academic and religious materials prove difficult to comprehend. One has sympathy with both priest and children, when the former describes his teaching difficulties in the Indian day school. "When I try to teach a catechism class, the children just look at me like fish. There is no comprehension in their faces."

In school, the Indian children by no means accept passively the restrictions put upon them or the rules and rebukes meted out. They appear not to understand the right to correct which the school authorities assume for themselves. One of the priests reported that an Indian boy had come to him to complain after one of the nuns (his teacher) had scolded him. "She insulted me!" the boy insisted. The nuns, on their part, find the children's resentment of authority trying. As one of them said, "I get tired of always handling these children with white gloves."

Resistance against the Kuper Island boarding school has more than once taken the form of dramatic attempts at escape. The story was told to me in the agency of one homesick boy who successfully rode a log across the five-mile body of water to the mainland. Two other boys attempted to make their way across in a canoe but were carried far out of their course and had to be rescued.

Such stories should not carry the implication of cruel treatment of the children in the boarding school. Actually, the boy who rode the log later grew to like the school. During the summer of 1954 he went back of his own accord, hoping to find odd jobs that would enable him to spend the summer there. Life in the Kuper Island boarding school, however, is a regimented one, as in many convent schools. Though the boys and girls attend classes together, they are rigidly segregated otherwise in living arrangements which are a far cry from the conditions of close family living on the reserve.

As the Indian children grow into preadolescence, they lose the unkempt look of early childhood, thanks partly to the efforts of the schools. Girls, particularly, of about ten, eleven, twelve, are capable of keeping themselves well-combed and clean. Frequently on my visits to homes during the summer vacation period, the presence of one of these neat and carefully dressed girls in the midst of the harum-scarum horde of younger children was almost startling. And the contrast was not only in clothing but in manner. The Camas girl of eleven is a responsible, poised young adult. She helps with housework, shares in the care of younger children, and takes a hand in the knitting. The making of the sweater sleeves may be entrusted to her, as her first step in learning the skill.

Because of these responsibilities, it is possible that the girl's life in these preadolescent years is more satisfying to her than the boy's is to him. Simply by being around the house, the girl learns the work role of women, in the tradition of the old days. But the boy no longer has a masculine model to attach himself to. His father and his grandfather are now away at work off in the sawmills or on the docks, and the boy is left at home, without tasks to do or skills to learn. He has long hours in the summer to fill only with play and wandering.

Both boys and girls are mingling more with White children than their parents did, and they are becoming more assertive in doing so. As one Indian grandfather said: "Why, when I was a boy, I wouldn't think of going up to talk to some White boys freely the way children do now. The feeling of the White people toward us is only just beginning to change." Though the Indian child, outside of school, is mainly confined to contacts with other Indians, still he is free to wander into town, buy candy and gum and comics in the White man's stores, and go to the movies. He can talk about Peter Pan with the White children who come down to his river to swim. He can join the Boy Scouts.

His contacts with White adults, as I know from personal experience, can be very generous and friendly, though sometimes tinged with defiance or unfriendly staring in the initial stages of acquaintance. There were children among the Camas who, after one or two contacts, would run to meet me with arms outstretched when they saw me approaching. In every home there were some children who responded to me at the outset with smiles and friendly curiosity. Occasionally gifts were offered, such as peppermints from the candy sacks. A little two-year-old in her first meeting with me proffered a long and beautiful spike of field grass.

This generous, outgoing behavior is one of the most noticeable characteristics of the Camas child. However, his personality in its easily observed aspects is perhaps best described by the word "independent"—if one may hazard a generalization about the children. From the two-year-old who manages to cut out a magazine picture with a safety pin, to the older boy who rides a log across five miles of water, the Indian child is all that independent implies: he is exploratory, resourceful, stubborn, daring, assertive, self-reliant, resistant toward authority.

It is impossible in a study of this kind to investigate thoroughly all aspects of this independence, or to discover all its roots. They are embedded in the complex interaction of organic, psychological, and social processes. Yet I have already pointed to some of the more obvious conditions that nurture this Camas personality. We have seen how the Indian child is exposed to certain attitudes that foster independence from birth. He is assumed by his mother to have autonomy even as an infant; and as a young child he is not only cherished but unthwarted, unpunished, and unrestrained in his exploration of his world. In granting him this freedom, his parents, I have suggested, may be partly motivated by expectations related to old beliefs or feelings about children; and they may be partly drifting ineffectually as disciplinarians, as the result of new roles forced upon them by a changing social structure. It should be remembered also that the parents themselves are independent in their own eyes. When they laughingly describe their children as "stubborn" in the presence of the children themselves, they are communicating a value related to the self-image. As Stephen T. Boggs has well put it, "One could suggest that parents love, encourage, discipline, or repress their children because children reflect what the self is or aspires to be, or what it should not be." [26]

It could also be suggested that the Camas children, as they live along with their individualistic parents, are taking on independent personal ways through the process of "absorption" that occurs, as Cora Du Bois has said, when behavior is "consistently observed in other members of the family." [27] If this is true today, it was no less true in the early days. The children of the Big House also absorbed the individualism of their elders. But there was a difference. This earlier individualism was conveyed through a smoothly functioning status system and a framework of authoritarian controls and taboos that imposed restraints. Today the neglected-looking Indian child is still absorbing the individualism of his parents, but it is an individualism modified by the changes that have come about. It is tinged with protest and affected by loss of the old mechanisms of control.

What lies ahead for this child? In our opening pages we heard him challenging, "So, you have come to look at the Indians?" Now, as we take leave of him, what can we answer? What must we say about the social processes that have brought him to this point in history? And what can we forecast for the future? There he goes, headed more certainly toward the new way than the old, since he is young. What will the new way hold for him? How new can it be?

26. Stephen T. Boggs, "Culture Change and the Personality of Ojibwa Children," *American Anthropologist* 60 (February 1958): 54.
27. Cora Du Bois, "Attitudes Toward Food and Hunger in Alor," in *Language, Culture, and Personality: Essays in Memory of Edward Sapir*, Leslie Spier, A. Irving Hallowell, and Stanley S. Newman, eds. (Menasha, Wis.: Sapir Memorial Fund, 1941), p. 272.

7

The New Way: Implications, Recommendations, Predictions

We have seen that beneath the external forms introduced by the White man, the old mechanisms of Camas social organization continue to operate. The land is divided into plots of ground, and single-family houses have been built upon them in Western community style, but a community in Western terms has not been formed. Needy relatives crowd into the small homes, where the grandmother still dominates; ties between close kin continue to form the basis of trust. An elective system of chieftainship and representation has been introduced, but its efficacy is small. Cooperation along lines which cut across kinship groupings is not yet well understood. The old potlatch system—the very keystone of the old economic and social structure—has been outlawed, but its vestiges remain in the present winter ceremonies. Livelihood is no longer linked with the land and the rivers and sea, but the old seasonal cycle of life endures. And more important, the values implicit in the old social structure continue to operate in the present. Lavish giving and spending are avenues to prestige today, as in the past. The White man's emphasis on saving and planning has not been learned, nor has his willingness to subordinate himself to the demands of a routinized, supervised life. The old social organization of the Camas Indians —that close-knit system of institutions and relationships—has retained much of its inner coherence. Life today for many proceeds on the basis of the old habits of association, linked and interlinked.

When we search for the reasons for the persistence of the system to this extent, two come to mind at once: policies of the church and the government have allowed the old ways to endure; and no alternatives offering comparable prestige satisfactions have been available. A social organization comprises a status system. When change is introduced, new and better avenues to status must be provided, if the intention is to remove the old foundations. As Malinowski has so well said:

> One kind of institution can be replaced by another which fulfills a similar function. But such change is difficult, and it always has to move toward something which is better in the cultural sense, that is, better endowed, giving greater scope and opportunities to the people who live in that institution. . . . For it is one of the soundest and most significant principles of social science that people are prepared to pass only from worse to better. Only such change is encompassed without much friction and with relative rapidity.[1]

In short, to remove the potlatch but to leave the Indian in poverty, dependent on the government and unable to step into the new society on an equal footing with the White man, courts failure. Under such circumstances the Indian prefers to remain an Indian, to bolster himself by such prestige mechanisms of the old society as he can preserve. In the case of the Camas, their very numbers and concentration on the reserve have made possible an intimate interdependence and have facilitated the preservation of the Indian institutions.

An instructive comparison is provided by the Menomini Indians of Wisconsin.[2] Though a native-oriented group exists

---

1. Bronislaw Malinowski, *The Dynamics of Culture Change* (New Haven: Yale University Press, 1945), pp. 52 and 56.
2. See George D. Spindler, *Sociocultural and Psychological Processes in Menomini Acculturation,* University of California Publications in Culture and Society, vol. 5 (Berkeley and Los Angeles: University of California Press, 1955).

among them, the old native ceremonials and values by no means constitute an over-arching system which touches the lives of most of the members of the tribe, as in the case of the Camas. On the contrary, Western values have become primary and the group enjoying highest status is the acculturated "elite" who interact exclusively with each other or with middle-class Whites in nearby towns. This has come about through the presence on the reserve of a flourishing lumber industry, Indian-owned and operated, making possible an income level for Indians comparable to that of members of the neighboring White communities. Furthermore, responsible self-government has been encouraged in various ways, including the allocation to an Indian advisory board of the right of review over budget.

The Camas Indians, by contrast, have had little prosperity, little political autonomy. Those among them who move successfully toward the White man's way do so against odds. In view of this situation, the fact that the Camas have been able to maintain many aspects of their old system has probably been a fortunate circumstance. I have used the metaphor of batter on a griddle to describe the slow process of change on the Camas Reserve. I have pointed out that a high degree of disorganization or conflict has been absent. In spite of the deleterious effects of drinking and poverty, the Camas have preserved secure affectional ties and a measure of self-respect in their own terms. It is where these are lacking that culture change is accompanied by disintegration.

I am not suggesting, however, that all has been for the best. I believe that "psychological equivalents" in terms of new institutions and values could have been offered to the Camas and that future policies call for much more than passive approbation while the social processes jog on. Years of protest indicate that the Indians themselves have been far from satisfied with their relations with the White man. And the time is approaching when the educated younger generations will find it impossible to take refuge in the old ways. New avenues must be found to provide those institutions that will offer greater scope and opportunities. There is no escaping a conclusion for the Indians which parallels that arrived at long ago by Malinowski for the Africans: "It is impossible either to develop the African on his own lines or to change him into a colored Westerner without leaving him a substantial margin of material prosperity, of political autonomy, and of civic rights."[3]

What steps, then, are the logical ones for the administration to take, as it turns to the task of widening the opportunities for the Camas? Let us examine first those steps which actually were taken between 1954 and 1957 by the new superintendent, whose intention clearly was to improve economic conditions, raise the status of the Indians in the eyes of the White population, and increase responsible decision-making. Economic improvement was evident in new housing, the electrification of the villages, and the instalment of city water mains in one of the remoter villages formerly completely dependent upon river water. These improvements were made possible largely by the superintendent's success in augmenting the band fund through better timber sales. The water mains, however, were put in with the cooperation of the town authorities and represented cooperation between Whites and Indians on a new level. The local newspaper on 25 April 1957 reported, "The city council intends to treat [Village II] Indians as ordinary customers, and to bill them monthly as with all other customers."

In other ways as well, the citizens of the town and the citizens of the reserve were brought closer. An unprecedented joint meeting of the Indian band council and the city council, to consider mutual concerns such as the beer parlor question, was favorably publicized in the local newspaper. Upon the formal occasion of the new mayor's first appearance in his official robes, Indian leaders were invited to participate. A photograph of the Indian chief and the mayor, standing side by side, both in "costume," appeared in the newspaper to commemorate the event.

The superintendent, between 1954 and 1957, supplied the newspapers with a good many news items relative to Indian

3. Malinowski, *Dynamics,* p. 71.

affairs. Some of these served the purpose of informing the public of new developments on the reserve. Others were probably calculated to present the Indian as a person whose life was as newsworthy as the White man's life. Photographs appeared of the winners of the Indian Girl's Club baby shows; an Indian woman was photographed knitting a sweater for the champion swimmer of the English channel; prizes won by Indian school children were announced, as were Indian marriages and deaths. Articles stressed the growing "self-help" that was being practised among the Indians and the "ever increasing voice in the governing of their own affairs."

The band council, indeed, was taking over more responsibility for deciding on how its funds and the moneys from the B.C. Special Fund should be spent; it was allocating the new houses; it was active in turning the course of the river on the reserve, to prevent the destruction of good land. It was building a garage to house the tractor it had acquired for use of the band; and by 1957 it was meeting twice a month instead of once a month, as in 1954, and plans were afoot for paying the chief and councillors a small fee for their services.

In many other ways the superintendent tried to put the Indian in a more favorable light in the eyes of the White man and to improve the conditions of his life. To combat the disorderly aftermaths of beer parlor drinking, an effort was being made to keep the worst offenders out of the beer parlors; and the Indian constable had become more active in trying to prevent trouble. He stationed himself outside of the beer parlors on Friday and Saturday nights. "When things get rough and folks are drinking, they call me in," he was quoted as saying in the newspaper article featuring him as local "citizen" in July 1957. "I generally manage to calm them down instead of calling the Mounties."

A further development of importance relative to the beer parlor problem was the end of discrimination. Under new management, the town beer parlor that was closed to Indians in 1954 had by 1957 changed its policies and was admitting all comers.

Not only had the appearance of the reserve been somewhat

improved by the erection of a number of new houses of modern design comparing favorably with new houses in the town but the appearance of many Indians themselves had been bettered by the agency's efforts to make false teeth available at little or no cost.

Finally, a definite step had been taken toward untangling the obscurities of land boundaries and Indian ownership. An expert from Ottawa arrived in the summer of 1957 to devote full time to the problem.

A newspaper item on 7 March 1957 carried the announcement that negotiations were progressing between the Camas Indians and Prevost Post No. 10 of the Native Sons of British Columbia not only to restore the old stone church on the reserve, but to allow the Whites access to it. Perhaps no more cogent evidence of improved relationships between Indians and Whites could possibly be produced. Standing in ruins on Indian land, the old church has been a bone of contention since the early days, a symbol of the Indian's proud defense of what he felt was his against the encroachment of the White man. That such a statement as the following could appear in the newspaper article marks a real turning of the tide: "Opposition to the Whites has been overcome now, it is reported, and talks are continuing on an agreement. . . ."

All these measures taken between 1954 and 1957 appear, at least on the surface, to be forward-looking steps. No one, surely, would quarrel either with the intentions behind them or with the results. However, questions remain to be asked. Are measures of this kind enough? Do they strike deeply enough at the heart of the problem? For example, though the new housing and the electrification of the villages appear to be improvements, one may still ask, was the *decision* that brought them into being made by the Indians themselves, or by the superintendent? I suggest that the basic need of the Indian for improved status will not be met until every possible step is taken to break his dependence on the government and to make him responsible for his own decisions, every step of the way.

Does this imply, perhaps, the immediate abolition of the

reserve system itself? Not necessarily. In fact, the history of the Camas people reveals their strong feeling of right to the land and of bitterness over encroachments that have already been made. To pull out from under them what security they have in their present land occupancy and privileges would seem to be an unwise move and a much too abrupt one. There are ways, however, in which the reserve system could be radically modified, or made more flexible, to encourage a great deal more independence in the Indian without drastically removing him from his familiar moorings in his present rights and habits. Some of these ways have been envisaged already, boldly proposed—not for the Camas specifically, but for the Indians of British Columbia in general—by Hawthorn, Belshaw, and Jamieson.[4] Indeed, at this point it becomes necessary to think beyond the Camas and their local superintendent, since many of the departures that might be recommended involve basic changes in the Indian Act and go beyond the domain of any local office.

Of especial importance in view of Camas findings is the Hawthorn, Belshaw, and Jamieson proposal that the tie between land ownership and occupancy be severed, to allow the Indian greater independence in terms of both occupational and geographic mobility. Indians would travel, it is believed, to other reserves and locales for work, if they could at the same time retain their privileges of land ownership and membership in their own bands. Such a provision would not only improve the employment situation and promote independence, but would tend at the same time to break up the isolation of the Indian as a conspicuous minority group on his reserve. The suggested mechanism for freeing the Indian from his present tie to the reserve is the formation of the members of the band into a "band corporation" holding the title to existing property and band funds. Greater mobility would also be facilitated, it is proposed, if the

---

4. H. B. Hawthorn, C. S. Belshaw, and S. M. Jamieson, *The Indians of British Columbia: A Study of Contemporary Social Adjustment* (Berkeley and Los Angeles: University of California Press, 1958). See chapters 29 and 30 for the proposals I am discussing.

tax status of the Indian were amended according to a principle that would make him, and not his property, tax-free.

My survey of the settlement pattern of the Camas Reserve revealed how widely the Camas travel outside of their own boundaries, even under the present restricting conditions. They visit relatives up and down the coast; they attend winter ceremonies and Shaker services in other locales both on the island and in the state of Washington; some of them even try life in the States on their own initiative. It is my prediction that they are ready for and would make use of opportunities offered by greater freedom of residence.

As greater mobility developed, it is suggested by Hawthorn, Belshaw, and Jamieson that the concept of the functions of the reserve might become so altered that there would eventually be no bars to admitting members of the White population to residence as tenants on reserve property. It is conceivable that this could happen on the Camas Reserve, since already the White man and the Indian are such close neighbors in those areas where the town and the other shopping centers border the reserve.

A modified view of property, it is further suggested, might also eventuate in the Indians'—as individuals or as a band—acquiring the right to own land outside of the reserve. Such land could be bought, sold, and used as security for capital-raising. In this way another avenue toward improved financial status would be opened.

It is unlikely that economic conditions can be much improved for the Indians, however, without special attention to the employment situation, on the part of the agency or specially appointed officers. Ways will have to be found to canvass work possibilities in the region, to keep informed of trends in the labor market, and to plan accordingly for increased technical and vocational training. The Camas have demonstrated their aptitude for mechanical work. But only one Camas man is employed at present as an auto mechanic, only a handful as carpenters. Ways to increase employment possibilities in these trades might be explored at the outset.

It cannot be emphasized too often that the giving of welfare assistance to alleviate poor economic conditions not only fails to solve the basic economic problem but promotes the dependence of the Indian, and accentuates the humiliation of his position. Because of the nature of the old Indian status system, in which lavish reciprocation for gifts received was always called for, if an individual expected to lay claim to any prestige, the Indian who receives welfare aid today is especially vulnerable to feelings of degradation. Perhaps these are lessened when all direct relief received can come from the band's own funds.

Can band councils be developed into instruments capable of highly responsible decision-making? Can they learn how to become responsible for welfare decisions and others of such importance as would be involved, for instance, in working out a system of allocation of land and registry of boundaries? Can they look forward to the time when experts from Ottawa will not have to be called in to disentangle boundary questions? The experience of the years 1954–1957 seems to indicate that the Camas band council has shown growth, not only in the scope of its decision-making but in its interest in its functions. Its greater growth in the future rests partly, of course, on the willingness of the government to allocate important decision-making to the councils. It rests also on the nature of the other changes that will gradually move the Indian, in all aspects of his life, closer to independence and equality with the White man, and greater participation in political affairs—his own and those of the larger community. Is there any reason why the Indian band could not have a representation on a town commission, for instance, to consider affairs of mutual concern? The recent joint meeting of city council and Camas band council points to the possible readiness of both town and Indian band for such cooperation.

And is there any reason, I must ask, for the continuance of denial to the Indian of the liquor rights enjoyed by the White man? Is there any point in even talking of increased responsibility and decision-making on the part of band councils, while the Indian, in respect to liquor rights, is still treated as a dependent? Let the band councils themselves tackle the problems of control of drinking, after the bans are lifted.

In this general move toward independence, the schools might play an increased part. This would require, of course, an appreciation on the part of teachers and school officials of the independence the Indian child has already had built into him, by the time he comes to school. It would require, as well, an understanding of the importance of turning it to positive uses, rather than considering it a manifestation to be trimmed down to the far too usual pattern of submissive school behavior. To teach children in a way that develops responsibility for controls and decisions and that capitalizes on resourceful assertiveness is the hard way, but one which educators believe lays the best foundation for democratic participation for all children. In the case of the Indian children, school experience in electing class officers, formulating classroom rules and plans, and in organizing and carrying out a program of responsible jobs for the school should be of especial value in individual development. Included among these jobs might be the operation of a school store and post office; mimeographing and distributing of school announcements; and for older children, taking certain responsibilities for helping out in the lower grades.

Furthermore, it would be particularly important for the Indian children to experience authority in school in its rational, nonarbitrary aspects, to help them learn the ways of self-discipline that are rooted in reason rather than defiance. I am not suggesting that teachers abdicate control, but rather that they make every effort to work with, rather than against, the child's need for autonomy, presenting themselves not as powers but as people who can be approached with problems, and as fair arbiters who earn the respect the children give them.

The use of the discussion method—with children and teacher sitting face to face engaging in honest probing—would be invaluable in encouraging the children to work their way through issues that arise relevant to disciplinary matters or indeed any other problems—personal, social, intellectual. There could be no better way to encourage questioning attitudes; to help children see that clarification can be arrived at through interchange of ideas; and to accustom children to responsible social participation in which everyone's contribution can count. Even first-graders can discuss questions of concern to them with great profit, learning in this way new skills and new confidence.

Of course, the Indian first-grader is greatly hampered if he comes to school irregularly, in poor health, and without the care that would give him a sense of being adequately dressed and groomed; or if he arrives speaking only his native language. If he cannot handle English, then his major learning in the early grades must necessarily become the learning of English. As long as there are children handicapped in this way and as long as it seems necessary to segregate some Indian children in Indian schools, special skill in language teaching should be required of teachers.

Indeed, teachers of Indian children ideally should be equipped with a number of special knowledges and skills if they are to contribute in an important way to the emergence of a new self-respect in the Indian. They need, in the first place, to *wish* to make this contribution. Without knowledge of the Indian's past or understanding of why his present life often appears to be such a shabby and primitive thing, this wish may be absent. Courses in general anthropology as well as studies in ethnic relations and local Indian cultures might profitably be included in their training.

Greater understanding of Indian life might affect teachers' attitudes not only toward the children but toward the parents, perhaps facilitating parent-teacher relations built upon trust and simple human respect. Such understanding also might help teachers make those adaptations of the Provincial curriculum which should be made, especially for the younger children, if their learning is to have some relation to the life they know, and consequently some relevance and meaning. Only such learning will speed them at the normal rate through the grades. And only such understanding on the part of teachers will lead to sensitive awareness of each child and his needs in relation to the problem of growing up in a changing culture. Some children may be able to move much more rapidly than others toward the ways and values of the White society, because of family approval and support. Others will move more slowly, and should move slowly, in order to avoid unnecessary conflict and to retain the strengths that family solidarity can provide. Perhaps it is self-evident that a problem of this scope calls for all the resourcefulness that can be brought to bear in solving it. To leave it exclusively in the hands of the White teachers and school administrators is not enough. Indian parents might contribute to its solution, if encouraged to make their voices heard as members of parent-teacher associations and even eventually as representatives on school boards.

I have already mentioned the efforts of the Catholic day school to organize activities for parents, especially the Mother's Club and Girl's Club. It would be profitable to explore a much fuller use of the school—Indian or public—as an educational center for parents. If Indians are to contribute to the school's endeavors for their children, the scope of their understanding of educational aims will have to be enlarged and ways of communicating facilitated. Mother's clubs are a step in the right direction, providing not only experiences in responsible participation, in themselves educational, but important new avenues for social expression. As the Indians move farther away from the forms of their old life, they will need many such substitutes for the old social satisfactions.

The school's role, of course, is no more than auxiliary; it can only help the Indian prepare to take those steps which the larger society will have to guarantee. It can equip him with the speech, the skills, the habits which make it easier for him to move toward and make the most of the autonomy and equality which must be granted by those in position to grant it, before basic change can occur.

It is not the role of the school, the White community, or the government to force change upon the Indian. It is the obligation of the White society, however, to make it possible for the Indian to exercise free choice and to achieve status as satisfactorily in the White man's terms as he now achieves it in his own through perpetuation of his old ways on the reserve.

At the heart of the web of a culture is the individual sustained by the family and community ways that give meaning to his life. Only by the substitution of new interpersonal satisfactions for old can the interlocking strands be made to loosen and to take on new forms and combinations. There can be no other starting point for administrators.

Is it possible to envision a terminal point? Is it within reason to anticipate a time when the Camas Indians will have become completely assimilated? Will they lose their identity as Indians and merge so entirely with the life of the town that they will become indistinguishable as a group? Prediction is hazardous, but nevertheless it is possible to point to reasons why assimilation to this extent may not take place, at least within the foreseeable future, though equal rights be granted and freedom and independence guaranteed.

Consider, in the first place, the nature of our Vancouver Island town as a community whose ways the Camas would share, if they and their homes were to become an integral part of it. Originating as a trading post serving the early British settlers, the town has gradually drawn in a diverse group whose ties are those of neighbors, not kin, and whose social pattern of living differs basically from that of the Camas. Though a small number of Sikhs and Chinese are represented in the population, the majority of the town residents are of British ancestry, united under the old English village tradition of neighborliness.[5] Even the adjoining northern area of scattered small communities and rural dwellings is incorporated as a district and is administered by an official whose title, "reeve," betrays the old English origin of the office. As neighbors, and not as kin, the residents of the town and the district come together to work for the common good, through such organizations as the Chamber of Commerce and the Rotary and Kiwanis clubs; as Protestants they are active, in varying degrees, in the congregations of their churches; they extend help to one another through the Knights of Pythias, the Odd Fellows, Moose, and Eagles, with their ladies' auxiliaries;

---

5. See George C. Homans, *English Villagers of the Thirteenth Century* (Cambridge: Harvard University Press, 1941).

and for recreation they seek out like-minded friends and form their little theater guild, choral group, riding club, sports club, and yacht club. Social interchange with neighbors, civic pride, concern for the welfare of others regardless of kinship ties—these form the core of interaction in the district and the town.

In contrast, picture Village I, partially abandoned for a quarter of each year, its houses standing about in the weeds, its occupants heedless of each other as neighbors in the daily round of living. Through what transformation could this community become one of the residential districts of the town, sharing its neighborly patterns and its town concerns? Transform the house of the Camas itinerant, make of his village a neighborhood, and his whole system of social interaction must be transformed.

As we know, the Camas villagers cannot and do not interact as neighbors partially because they are too busy visiting their kin, in the way that was established in an early day when only kinfolk could be trusted and depended upon to provide assistance. We know, too, that the Camas house stands in its crude, half-abandoned condition partially because such a dwelling is functional and has always been functional in relation to the Camas social system as a whole. Needing little care, it frees its owners to travel in the customary round; and it reflects a set of customs related to the status and role of the wife. Make of the Camas house a town house and the whole structure of Camas marital relations must be changed. Indeed, those Indian women who now accompany their husbands to the beer parlors and elsewhere for recreation may not learn to stay at home, tending houses and gardens, chatting with clubwomen, and caring for children, until such time as their husbands want them to.

The pattern of Camas Village life, then, has deep roots in habits of association, in functions, and in sentiments that have grown up around the customary ways. It may be unrealistic to expect these habits to disappear entirely, leaving no trace in the preferred style of community living that may develop in the future. The strength of the system as a whole, its parts complexly interlinked, must be reckoned with. To be sure, the web of Camas culture is changing and will continue to change. We have already seen evidences of some neighborly action: there is the Mother's Club made up of individuals who do not have close kinship ties and there are the beginnings of a burial association in which aid is extended to all in the band. New ways will come, but they will come more rapidly to some of the villagers than to others; and vestiges of the old system of interpersonal relations may remain indefinitely. Indeed, distinctive settlement patterns and habits of social organization have been known to persist for centuries, despite the close proximity of other ways of life—as in the Welsh countryside, for instance, where a diffuse type of rural settlement based on early tribal organization has prevailed without signs of disintegration until recently, in spite of the early introduction of towns by alien influences.[6] There seems to be no compelling reason to believe that the town pattern as exemplified on Vancouver Island represents a form of community living which the Camas must inevitably adopt in the future.

It is true that rapid and radical change in ways of living sometimes occurs. The Manus of New Guinea, according to Margaret Mead's recent report,[7] have precipitously abandoned their primitive life as water dwellers in order to adopt land settlement and new external forms of social organization based on present-day Western practices. An especially favorable set of circumstances made this rapid change possible, including the presence of a gifted leader who was able to make the most of a strategic moment. Equally crucial was this fact: life in the primitive culture had been characterized by "a driving discontent with things as they were."[8] The opportunity for change was seized because the new order promised a way out of the pressures and dissatisfactions of the old life.

No such set of circumstances characterizes Camas life. The older Indians of the band look back with nostalgia on an early

---

6. Alwyn D. Rees, *Life in a Welsh Countryside: A Social Study of Llanfihangel yng Ngwynfa* (Cardiff: University of Wales Press, 1950).
7. Margaret Mead, *New Lives for Old: Cultural Transformation—Manus, 1928–1953* (New York: William Morrow and Company, 1956).
8. Ibid., p. 158.

culture that may have been close to a "genuine" one in Sapir's use of the term—a culture "inherently harmonious, balanced, self-satisfactory." [9] Even the younger people today, though they are beginning to turn their backs on the ceremonies and supernatural beliefs of the old society, continue to enjoy aspects of its old system of social relations—its summer trips to the berry fields, its frequent contacts with the closely related kinship groups.

The pattern of community living that will develop for the Camas Indian in the future may be unlike either the present Indian village pattern or the pattern of the town. The habit of travel may continue to exert its appeal, and a new mobile residence pattern may take shape, particularly if Ottawa makes provision for loosening the present tie to the reserve. If this happens, new needs may arise, calling into being new institutions. For example, new mechanisms providing for group solidarity and support may be necessary for at least a time, to supplant the functions of the smaller band gatherings in the winter and to give some sense of unity and identification to a people less rooted than they were before. The present large Indian organizations, the Native Brotherhood of British Columbia and the North American Indian Brotherhood, may take on changed significance as associations providing ties wherever residence may be. Other larger-than-local associations may come into being, perhaps growing out of the present larger-than-local winter dance gatherings; or churches may extend their functions. Indeed, the Shaker church already offers ties that cross over from reserve to reserve, up and down the coast. Conceivably it could expand its influence, growing and changing with the times.

The Camas Indian, even as he moves closer to the life of the White neighbor—trying out the mother's clubs and enjoying the television and water mains that are part of the public domain—may retain group solidarity and a core of his own ways, in the manner of other ethnic groups in America. In his case, this core

9. Edward Sapir, *Culture, Language and Personality: Selected Essays* (Berkeley and Los Angeles: University of California Press, 1957), p. 90.

may remain a very solid one, shaping much of the life he chooses to live both in private and in public.

The task of the administrator, at every point as the old gives way to the new, is to be aware of the anatomy of the social system he is dealing with; to be cognizant of the interplay of all the elements that are its parts; to be creative in envisaging the psychological equivalents that may be offered; and to be receptive to new developments in modern community living which may be uniquely Indian in their origin. The task, of course, is not his alone. I reiterate, Indians will move successfully into modern life as they themselves develop leaders and as they themselves make the important decisions, every step of the way.

Epilogue: Summer 1968

A return to the reserve in 1968 reveals that steady progress has been made in the march toward equal sharing of rights and privileges. Though there have been no basic changes in the reserve system itself, the new gains are significant. For example: The Indian is no longer denied the White man's liquor rights; young people are more easily finding employment in the town—in banks, stores, offices, and gas stations; and Indian parents whose children attend Provincial schools now have the right, along with other parents, to vote for school boards and even to seek election as school trustees.

Yet, while these and other changes have been taking place, many of the old problems have persisted, such as the drinking ending in violence, the flood of requests for relief after the summer trips to the berry fields, and the casual attitudes of many men toward steady employment. Furthermore, the reserve itself has changed very little in outward appearance. The first impression is that almost nothing has happened in these intervening years to alter the basic Indian way of life.

Our task now is to try to discover to what extent this first impression holds, upon closer observation. Is it true that the Camas Indian is remaining an Indian as time carries him forward? Are any new developments in preferred style of living discernible?

EPILOGUE

I propose that we begin with a look at the villages themselves. What we learn will lead us to the questions that are crucial to explore.

First, we note that the old cluttered houses of 1954 and 1957 are, if anything, more cluttered and dilapidated, though television is more in evidence than formerly. Old abandoned cars now stand about in a number of yards and add to the look of neglect. A few houses that were in extremely bad condition in 1957 have collapsed or have been taken down and all traces removed. True, a great many new houses have been built for the younger generation on the parents' property, since the population has increased by five hundred since 1954. The large open space in the middle of Village I is no longer so open. New one-story houses for the young Gordons and others are crowding in. These new homes, wherever they may be built on the reserve, have not yet accumulated clutter. Is this because accumulation takes time, or because the houses are built without porches to hold tires, boxes, and bottles, or because the younger generation really wants to live another way? However it may be, most of these dwellings stand in the weeds, splattered with dirt, and appear not radically out of place in the general picture of poverty and neglect.

And what of our three families and their homes? The Paul Harrys continue to live as before, sheltering a large clan of children and grandchildren in their camp-like house, blackened with age and now falling into ruin. "Our house has been condemned, the boards are all rotten," Mr. Harry explains.

Margaret Gordon, on her upward climb toward a better life, has moved with her husband and children to a farmhouse in comparatively good condition, just off the reserve. Of course, by this move she loses her Indian privileges of vote and welfare, but she has chosen this way for the sake of her children.

The Wilson house begins to show the effects of age, and in this respect it looks more Indian than it used to. Is this partly because Mrs. Wilson, the industrious housewife, has been dead now for a number of years? The remaining family members still living there continue to take leadership positions in Indian affairs. Mr. Wilson served a recent term as chief, and one of his children was elected to this position a few years earlier and still fills an important office in the band council.

The Shakers have prospered sufficiently to be able to erect a new small brick church. It stands a little distance from the site of the former church, and the old church itself has been moved beside it to serve as a dining hall. Comments of my informants indicated no significant change in the importance of the Shakers in the Camas local affairs.

Our Canadian town appears to be encroaching slightly on the reserve. The old quiet trunk road along which Indian houses used to stand is now lined with commercial enterprises—a bank, a beauty parlor, a filling station, a shopping center. Those on the Indian side of the street lease the land from the Indian owners, and all but one of the old Indian houses have been taken down or moved away.

And actually there are other evidences of change—other buildings or groups of buildings that call for comment, now that we have said that in general the reserve looks much the same. In themselves they may seem relatively insignificant, but we can take them as concrete symbols of four developments important to explore. These are the buildings: First, a well-designed, two-room frame structure on reserve land near the town, to house the band council office; secondly, a new housing project or "subdivision"—as yet unfinished—consisting of twenty frame dwellings arranged in precise rectangular order, standing in a secluded spot on the reserve not far from Villages I, II, and V; third, two new schoolhouses, one a large Catholic elementary school just outside of town and close to reserve land, a school that is now forty percent Indian, sixty percent White; the other a public elementary school, accessible to at least some of the children in Villages I, II, and V; and finally, in the large open space of Village I a huge, barn-like Big House for winter dances, constructed by the Indians themselves in the old style, with a hole in the roof for smoke from the fires.

Let us now look more closely at these new structures and the developments related to them.

The Band Council Office

This compact, attractive modern building where the band council now holds its meetings announces clearly the existence of the council and its increased autonomy as a decision-making body. No longer does a small inarticulate group gather around the superintendent in the privacy of his office twice a month. Instead, the council, increased to twelve members and organized into eight committees, meets weekly. The superintendent attends the meetings with the understanding that he comes at the council's request. Two of the leadership positions—that of secretary-treasurer and band manager—now require full-time work, and a sizable salary is paid by the Indian Affairs Branch to these two officers. All other members of the council, including the chief, receive small token amounts.

And what is the nature of this work that now demands such an increase in time and effort? In general we can say that the small beginnings toward responsibility-taking that were evident in 1957 have now become much more impressive attempts to manage, govern, and decide—within limits, of course, since the ultimate control remains in the hands of the Indian Affairs Branch. For example, the management of the new subdivision has been placed squarely in the hands of the council, along with responsibility to settle frictions arising between council and city over taxes collected from city enterprises leasing Indian land. Also, the Indians have themselves called in an expert for help in organizing an agricultural cooperative.

These developments are at least partly the result of a consistent effort on the part of the government to foster Indian initiative through a number of avenues. Prominent among these is the Community Development program, now four years old. Under its provisions, a Community Development Officer—the present one is an Indian—moves into the reserve to promote the organization of projects which the Indians can then sponsor and carry out. Among the most successful have been the adult education classes and the nursery school, both sponsored by the education committee of the band council. There will be more to say later about these two developments.

Suffice it to point out now that the Camas Reserve has been fortunate not only in its Community Development program, but in its two executive leaders on the band council—the secretary-treasurer and the band manager. Perhaps no amount of encouragement on the part of the Indian Affairs Branch would have been effective without the existence of this leadership potential among the Indians themselves. The secretary-treasurer and the band manager—one age thirty-seven, the other forty-four—are highly competent individuals, commanding respect among both Indians and Whites, and able to take a place in affairs that reach beyond the Camas Reserve. The manager, for instance, recently attended a week-long leadership conference held in the interior of British Columbia, a conference organized and run entirely by Indians from a number of British Columbia reserves. Also, as a panelist at a workshop in Vancouver, he helped to author a report for the B. C. Commission for the International Year for Human Rights, in which numerous suggestions are offered for the improvement of Indian life. Speaking of him, one of his cousins—a woman who was one of my earliest friends on the reserve—said: "He's a big man now. We're all proud of him."

This is not to suggest, however, that the council has overcome all of its old problems, or that it is functioning as a model of efficiency. In the eyes of Indians who are not on the council, it can seem both slow and inept. A woman, for instance, who was eager to move her family into the new subdivision, had been unable to get the key. "We were told to go to Johnny Gordon, but he said to go to Joe James; but Joe James says it's Johnny Gordon we should see. So what do we do? We were told we could move in three months ago." And a public school administrator reported that he and his colleagues have had only varying degrees of success in working with the education committee of the band council. He felt, moreover, that there were just a few leaders in the council, showing up on every committee and not welcoming others in their group.

But in spite of problems like these—familiar to us, as we recall the past history of the council—we can say that there has been steady movement among the Indians toward more self-direction. And there has been movement toward the establishing of working links with other Indians (non-kin) in other reserves. As a matter of fact, the fifteen bands managed by the Camas Agency have now formed the Southern Vancouver Island Tribal Federation. This cannot be considered a strictly non-kin organization, since—as we already know—the Camas Indians have close kin up and down the island. But it does represent a new effort at cooperation and concerted action, calling for the discipline of regular meetings of elected representatives. The strength of such an organization, as it develops and feels its power, could be very significant. Actually, one young Camas Indian who discussed this federation with me toward the end of my stay said that with its backing all the band councils and chiefs in the agency had just resigned, to protest the plan of the Minister of Indian Affairs to ask the band councils to administer their own social welfare. "We have no one trained enough to do it." The young man happened to be misinformed, as he seemed to be about a number of things. The important point, however, is that he visualized such action on the part of the federation as not only suitable but quite possible.

The Camas Indians, then, have in these intervening years taken very visible steps in learning how to act on their own behalf, and how to feel their political and social power. Even though the old reserve remains and still presents many of the same problems, there is movement toward new expectations, new skills.

The Subdivision

The subdivision, designed with the help of experts called in by the band council, at this stage looks more "White" than "Indian." Nowhere else on the reserve are there Indian houses standing this close together, or built side by side with such precision of order. The rectangle formed by the houses is exact. Indeed, the reader has only to visualize the pattern of small housing developments across the country in city after city.

EPILOGUE

The twenty houses are as yet unfinished, unpainted; some are still in the construction stage. But the plan is clear: The houses are one-story; each has a front and back door without porches; each has a car-port at the side; wiring and appliances are in. Five families, in fact, are already in residence. The hope had been to construct a few larger houses to accommodate the larger families, but due to cutting of budget by the Indian Affairs Branch, this was not possible. The plan remains to extend the project when more money becomes available. Applications are accepted from anyone who wishes to apply, and a priority list is established on the basis of need.

The question comes to mind at once: Does the subdivision symbolize a growing wish on the part of the Indians to live in a way that does not divide them noticeably from the citizens of the town? Does it represent a concrete step toward the White pattern of living? The answer to this must take into consideration, first of all, the underlying economic motive: young Indian families without property need houses; houses need running water; and water mains are expensive to install when dwellings are scattered. Ostensibly, then, the subdivision represents planning in realistic terms regarding modern facilities. If the result is leading to a typically "White" pattern, this may be an inevitable outcome rather than the expression of a major motive. One can only surmise that some of the Indians may be pleased to see this White housing pattern taking shape, particularly when they tell you—apparently with pride—that there is a plan afoot to "straighten up" and pave the roads of Village I after water mains have been installed; and also when they express their own eagerness to move in. But others are less pleased with the idea of the project, for a variety of reasons. For instance, two families living in the flats village were reported to have feelings of reluctance about moving up to the vicinity of the town. And a Village I resident, a woman of thirty-six, raised objections to the closeness of the houses. "I'd rather be off by myself where I couldn't hear all my neighbors' parties. There's a lot of partying there right now." Still another woman, this one a few years older, likewise felt that the houses were too close together. "You couldn't keep your place neat. There will be cluttered families moving there. . . . And the people in the subdivision wouldn't want me there since I drink only 7-Up and go to church."

The subdivision is obviously an experiment too new to assess at this early stage. That it represents a radical departure in the Indian pattern of living is clear. How successful it will be can only be conjectured. I feel that there is little point in hazarding a guess; and let me add this impression: I believe there are Indians on the band council who do not want to hear any comments from the Whites on this subdivision at the present time. Indeed, one of the Indians in a position to give me permission to go into the new houses withheld this permission and also seemed reluctant to talk with me. "There's been so many people around looking at the subdivision we're not giving permission now for people to go in." And this from an Indian who had been especially friendly to me on my three previous visits to the reserve, and especially eager to give me information about the Camas way of life!

It seems possible that now, as the Indians find themselves in closer contact with the White residents of the town and as they see themselves taking on more of the White patterns of living, the situation may be one of conflict for them. They are still unable to aspire to middle class White standards of interior housing—standards that are becoming increasingly familiar to them through the television now available to all—and so cannot escape feelings of sensitivity to White criticism. One of the ways to deal with this, of course, is to affirm proudly, "We are Indian!" The presence and strength of this urge toward affirmation of Indian status is a fact we have been aware of among the Camas all along. We shall see, as we proceed with the picture of 1968, that the urge is still present and powerful, indeed still activating a way of life.

The Indian, then, who was reluctant to admit the White anthropologist to the housing project may have been saying, "Leave us alone; this is our project; we'll do it our own way." If personal factors were involved—such as a desire to test power or to stand by possible statements made earlier against White research—these can never be fully known. The fact remains: Permission was not granted by the Indian to the White woman.

As we turn now to look at the new developments in schooling, it will become evident that Indian contact with Whites is indeed on the increase, especially among the children.

New Schools

The policy of the Indian Affairs Branch, initiated a few years ago, is to gradually bring about the end of segregation of Indian children in Indian schools. Our Camas children may now attend the old Catholic Indian day school only through fourth grade. Transfer is then necessary either to the new Catholic elementary school serving both Indians and Whites—and limiting the number of Indians it will accept—or to the public schools of the district. Boarding schools are still available, but the Kuper Island school has become a hostel offering care only. For their classes the children are ferried daily to the nearest public schools on Vancouver Island.

Does this mean, then, that our Indian children—in greater numbers than before—are now moving along side by side with the White boys and girls, enjoying the advantages of equal education and a new shared companionship? The situation is not that simple. True, a few parents expressed satisfaction that their children were "in with the White children," as one of them put it. But conversations with two public school administrators revealed that the situation is full of problems and frustrations for many Camas children. "What is there in it for Indian children when they enter public schools at grade four or five already behind, with poor health, poor hearing, and poor talking skills?" The facts are that approximately twenty-five percent of the Indian children have hearing difficulties, a higher proportion than among the White children; many come to school without breakfast and bring no lunch; and poor attendance is a major problem. The old situation persists: children are taken out of school when their parents go off to follow the harvest; they stay home and sleep late during the winter dance season; and they are kept at home to baby-sit whenever parents need baby-sitters. Interestingly enough, inability to speak English is no longer one of the handicaps. The coming of television may have helped the children with their learning of the language.

The problem is not one of basic intelligence. At age six the Indian children hold their own with others, and even test higher than White children in skills requiring good coordination. The falling-off begins after age six, and under the present system there is often no catching up.

The "present system," as the administrators explained, is one in which there simply is not enough budget for remedial work—a problem familiar to educators everywhere. Only one special class in an elementary school in the town can take Indian children who have fallen far behind—and what is one in the face of such need? The children simply have to trail along in the regular classes until they reach junior high age. Then they can be transferred to the many available three-year occupational courses that try to build up reading and language skills and give practical training on a job. The "present system," too, as one of the administrators put it, has not really formulated very well its aims for both Indian and White children. "Education should be concerned with thinking, finding things out. The acquisition of facts means nothing." Here, of course, he has touched upon one of the central problems for educators throughout Canada as well as the United States.

Under this system, then, many Camas children now attending public schools are struggling along. Some do make it all the way to high school graduation, as in the past. This year, for instance, there were three Indians among the public high school graduates. An Indian mother commented with pride on this figure, remarking that the Indian children rarely go this far. A father, whose children had made it part of the way and then dropped out, explained that his daughter "just couldn't get over that eighth grade hump," and his son, who started in high school, "couldn't keep going, couldn't keep interested."

A final quote from one of the administrators expresses frustration but points the way to remedial steps that in the end may greatly improve the situation. "I'm not sure I believe in integrated education when it means the Indian kids have to struggle in a class where they stand out as being so backward and inferior. If only they could get a better start at four and five." The facts are that kindergartens were introduced in the public schools in the area a year ago—though the children are not bussed in—and that one is also available now at the Indian day school; and that in 1965 the nursery school project for Camas children was funded by the Indian Affairs Branch, which is now making its greatest expenditures for education; also that for three years under the public school system, an "orientation class" has been available each year for approximately sixteen needy children between the ages of six and ten. These significant projects—especially the nursery school and the orientation class—are but drops in the bucket; but if they can be expanded to reach more children they may point the way to lessening some of the present sense of failure surrounding the experience of school for many Camas children.

The orientation class—held in an old public school building near Villages II and V—is designed to give physical care and training to those children who need above all to learn something about grooming, washing, and using flush toilets; or children whose needs for hot lunches and sleep are paramount. An Indian girl—a high school graduate from a family well known to the Camas—has been employed as a teacher-aide. It is the hope that after a period of no more than two years of this orientation, the children may be able to move on to the grades where they belong. Actually, in its three-year history four children have been able to go on to normal classes.

It would seem that there is a crying need for more orientation of this nature. However, objections are sometimes raised by parents. Here, perhaps, we are encountering another manifestation of the spirit of "We are Indian!" Though the hot lunches are universally appreciated, the washing of clothes and the showers are not. Feelings of insult may be involved; and some of the parents make it clear that they do not want to be called "White lovers" who take baths. Let us table this fact about Indian feeling for the time being. We will return to it before the end of our discussion.

The nursery school has given Camas mothers and four-year-old children new experiences in cooperation and education. After a short and unsuccessful beginning with a volunteer teacher, a young White woman with teacher-training qualifications was employed. All the management details, including allocation and spending of the funds, were in the hands of the mothers, who elected a parent chairman to keep things moving. The mothers of the twenty-four children who were enrolled were expected to volunteer their help one day a month, while a young Indian girl was hired as a permanent helper. The goals of the nursery school definitely did not center around washing the children ("though a mother would occasionally take the initiative to clean up a child who needed it, since there were many visitors and some were critical," the teacher explained). Rather, the goals were those of good nursery school programs everywhere: to give the children a sense of being accepted just as they are; a sense of confidence as they meet this first school experience; to help them learn to play together; to offer them good play equipment and materials they should become familiar with before entering kindergarten or first grade. ("Some of the children didn't know their colors; some had never seen scissors or a crayon.") They were taken on trips to broaden their experiences ("some didn't know what a chicken was"); and they were given language kits containing pictures of familiar objects.

This was the basic blueprint. Stated thus it gives no idea of the actual difficulties involved in getting the program under way and keeping it operating—a dramatic story that could well fill a book. Not all of the problems were related to the fact that this was a Camas Indian nursery school; some are commonly encountered wherever there is reliance on volunteer mother helpers; others can be expected wherever a new experiment in cooperation is launched among a proud and independent people. Certainly my own experience in establishing a nursery school for Tennessee mountain children many years ago brought me face to face with similar vicissitudes.[1]

1. Claudia Lewis, *Children of the Cumberland* (New York: Columbia University Press, 1946).

EPILOGUE

Of particular pertinence to us here are these following excerpts from the Camas nursery school story: When in the beginning the funds were slow in coming through and there was no money to pay the teacher, the parents held rummage sales and raised the money to pay her. And when they decided they wanted a Christmas program, they found a way to make all the necessary costumes for the children. We have seen before, particularly in relation to our discussion of the winter dances, that Camas Indians have a good deal of organizational skill and ability to make things happen when they want them to happen. Yet the fact remains that interest in the nursery school fell off after the early days when the parents were so involved in getting it under way. It was hard to keep the mothers coming for their day of volunteering. Many of them simply did not get up in the morning in time, and the children were sometimes dragged out of bed by the bus driver. The daily attendance fell from about twenty-four to twelve. And there were personality frictions. Was one of their parent chairmen too dominating for them? Was a barrier set up because she was Protestant and they were Catholic? Or was the trouble due to dislike of some of her relatives, who were among the more successful members of the Camas in mingling with White people? Housing the nursery school presented other difficulties. In the beginning, a new young Protestant minister offered his church hall (located just outside of the town) and even enrolled his own two children. This seemed an auspicious start. The headquarters were pleasant and the presence of three White children—one of them the teacher's son—gave the school an integrated character. "The Indian mothers treated the children all the same," the teacher reported. But this situation ran into difficulties in a few months. Dignitaries of the church ultimately found the "Indian smell" objectionable—as it was reported—and felt that the church premises should not be used for such a project. Therefore the school was asked to move. Fortunately one of the other Protestant churches, situated close to the border of the reserve, offered a room where the school still operates.

In the summer of 1968 the parent chairman canvassed the reserve, visiting every family where there were four-year-olds, to see if the parents wished to continue the school. A total of about fifty families signed up; certainly an indication that in spite of the fact that not all may end in cooperating, the parents do believe in the idea of the school, and want to try to support what is good for their children.

Another new effort to help the Indian children with their schooling was the after-school study program jointly sponsored by the Indian Affairs Branch and the school district. For one hundred nights during 1967–68 Indian children attending the high school—this includes children outside the Camas Reserve—were bussed in four nights a week to the school, where typewriters and other equipment were made available, and teachers were on hand to give study help.

The public school administrator who described the program to me felt that it had been extremely successful. Yet, he said, when questionnaires were sent to the parents asking if they would like to see the program continued, only six out of thirty-eight were returned. This, of course, may indicate not lack of interest but lack of ability to handle written questionnaires. A house-to-house canvass might have brought quite different results.

Still another effort on behalf of the children resulted in the establishment of a "receiving home" where neglected children are cared for until better arrangements are made for them. Promoted in the beginning by the Community Development Officer, the idea soon took hold. Six of the Camas women staged a "march" to Victoria—as it was described in the Indian Office—to request aid. (The women had not actually "marched"!) As a result someone was sent to study the situation for three months; the receiving home was set up; and now it functions with an Indian woman at its head.

Finally, but not least important, are the adult education classes requested and instituted three years ago by parents themselves, with the help of the Community Development Officer. Two teachers, one of them the nursery school teacher, undertook to teach grades one through eight in night classes held at first in the Band Hall and then in a school off the reserve.

("That was really quite a venture," one of the teachers said, "getting them to go off the reserve like this! They had a car pool.") An Indian girl was hired as an assistant and given some preliminary training in a three-day adult education conference in Vancouver.

The students who came to these classes—perhaps no more than fifteen or twenty at any one time—were Camas adults of all ages. One seventy-four-year-old woman, an owner of a good deal of property, wanted to know how to sign her name in connection with her leases. She enrolled in the school, learned to write her name fluently, and completed grade one. A man of about the same age, well known to everyone in the band, completed grade three; a band council member graduated from grade eight; and one of Paul Harry's daughters—now a young widow—improved her reading and spelling sufficiently to carry her through grade seven.

In addition to grade school classes, the Indian language was taught, at the request of the Indians—another piece of evidence, perhaps, of a continuing, if not growing, desire to remain Indian while at the same time moving along with the demands of modern life.

In connection with this discussion of schooling, it is important to mention also the efforts made by the Indian Affairs Branch to provide vocational training for adults who need it, as well as for the young people. A band council member, a man in his early fifties, reported that he was soon going north for some training in the laying of water mains so that he could work at these improvements when he returned to the Camas Reserve. Another middle-aged man had been sent away for a nine-month course in the handling of heavy machinery. However, he was not making use of this at the present time because he had begun to carve totem poles and small masks and figures for the tourist trade, and was finding this very lucrative work. Indeed, the Indian Affairs Branch was aiding these carving efforts, making it possible for him as well as for two other carvers in the Camas Band to travel to the United States to exhibit their products.

Camas children, as they move along through school against many odds, may in the long run find themselves in a more auspicious position than many other Canadian Indian children, for whom education is meaningless because unrelated to the pursuits, roles, and needs of the adults who are their models.[2] Here on the Camas Reserve, the Indian children are beginning to see Indian adults—well past youth—valuing and finding ways to obtain both grade school and vocational education. And another new circumstance is in the favor of our Camas children. The logging companies and some of the sawmills are now requiring twelfth grade of their new applicants. For this reason, many of the young people who are headed toward logging and the mills—the traditional work of their fathers and grandfathers, along with longshoring—may feel a new incentive to finish school.

We have said little so far about the question of discrimination in the schools. In 1954 and 1957 we found no evidence that Indian children did not receive equal treatment. We heard no expressions of complaint from Indian parents. Of course, this involved only a handful of children then attending schools that were largely White.

The picture in 1968 cannot be presented in such simple terms. An array of comments from both Indians and Whites reveals the existence now of a whole range of feeling. At one end of the scale are those comments indicating satisfaction with the situation and giving no hint of feelings of discrimination. An Indian father, for instance, whose younger children attend the new public elementary school at the edge of the town (ten percent Indian) said his children had been reluctant to go at first but found they were accepted and made friends with the White children. "There are a couple of White children come to the house to play. My kids like them even better than some of their Indian neighbors." And a man who had taught in this elementary school also attested to no feeling among the White

---

2. See H. B. Hawthorn, ed., *A Survey of the Contemporary Indians of Canada,* 2 vols. (Ottawa: Indian Affairs Branch, 1967), 2: 19–22.

children against the Indians. Furthermore, his own attitudes were very positive. He described the Indians as attractive children who in fact were more "open, generous, and spontaneous" than the White children.

But at the other end of the scale are the comments of the two public school administrators, who said they suspected there are Indian children who feel a lot of discrimination. "Kids in the high school feel left out if they can't dress like the others—particularly the girls who can't come all dressed up in the party-like clothes the others wear. And some teachers don't feel as accepting toward them as toward the White children." This comment touches upon the subtle matter of "feeling accepting"—or nonaccepting—which indeed may lead to thoughtless, insensitive treatment of children rather than out-and-out discriminatory practices. Instances of what might have been insensitivity were reported by one Indian mother who resented the way a teacher spoke to other teachers about "the two Indians" in her class, categorizing them thus and not bothering to use their names. This same mother was incensed, too, that a school principal should remark in the presence of the children that "the Indians don't go past sixth grade." And we might ask, was it "insensitivity" that led the church dignitaries to object to the presence of the nursery school children in their church hall?

In addition to these two ends of the scale, there is another dimension to explore. How do the Indian children react to what they may consider discriminatory attitudes? According to one of the administrators, they tend to stick together, and will beat up those of their own number who seem to be moving too close to the White children. ("We are Indian!" "We are Indian!"—again the proud defense.) Perhaps this is related to what we have already heard about the reluctance of the adults to go off the reserve for their adult education classes. Moving bodily into the White domain presents its difficulties. And indeed, we know that there are parents who must be conveying to their children that it is not good to be "White lovers." A few, in fact, according to a young White woman who had known Indian boys and girls as classmates, teach their children that "White people are bad." "But if you accept them they accept you," she added, referring to the children, "and there's no difficulty."

The fact that there are sometimes difficulties leads us straight to the question of the significance of the new Big House in Village I. Actually, the plan to construct this building was already in evidence in 1957. Tall posts had been hauled in and deposited on the site. When I returned in 1965, I saw the completed building. In 1968 all informants agreed that this Big House was indeed an active center for dances throughout the winter months.

A New Big House for the Old Ceremonies

Clearly, the winter dance ceremonies are by no means fading out as the Camas Indians find themselves in closer contact with the residents of the town. There are still Indians who do not attend; yet new dancers are being initiated each season, and the participants in the ceremonies are by no means limited to the elderly who are thoroughly committed to the old ways. For instance, a young teacher-aide was recently married in the Big House, in the traditional Indian style, and a naming ceremony was given by one of the more acculturated Indians who is very active in the band council. Among the dancers themselves are a number of the nursery school mothers, as well as the newly married teacher-aide.

The dances retain the features described earlier: new dancers are still helped to find a "song" and are expected to practically camp in the Big House throughout the winter season, dancing almost nightly; portraits are shown of deceased kin; payments are made for "helping," and gifts are given lavishly. All who dance do so in a possessed state, with faces painted.

Recent Camas initiates include a man of seventy-six and his son of forty-two, as well as a number of "school girls," as they were described in the Indian Office. "Don't the young girls dread to be taken?" I asked the nursery school teacher, who had been invited to some of the dances. "And don't the young people tend to think these dances are 'crazy'?" I added, remembering some of the remarks of earlier years. "No, they consider it an honor to be snatched, even though it's physically exhausting. The dances go up and down in favor. Right now they're up." She described the above-mentioned Indian wedding, which she had recently attended. "People gave talks in Indian about how to live. Blankets were given away and masks were used, because this family has the masks."

One of the former Camas chiefs spoke approvingly of the return of the mask dances. "They were dying out for a while, but now people seem to be having them a lot for weddings, funerals, and namings. My auntie died recently and they had mask dancing at the home before the funeral. I liked this."

The conclusion is inescapable that for the Camas one of the means for achieving psychological support and a sense of status is still through participation in the old ceremonies; for the basic situation has not changed. The Camas Indians are still inferiors in the eyes of the White population and dependents in the eyes of the government, despite the gains they have made in the sharing of privileges and the ability to make decisions about their own affairs.

We have seen already that some of the children are moving with difficulty into the integrated schools. The same can be said about the current employment situation. In spite of the general headway that has been made against discrimination, Indians still may encounter prejudice when they look for jobs. The logging companies, for instance, still have some feeling against hiring them, because of the well-known Indian habit of not showing up regularly on the job—the habit, that is, of some though not all Indians. And girls may run into difficulties. A member of the band council described a recent incident: "A while back some Indian girls were refused employment as salesgirls in one of the big stores on the trunk road. Members of the Mika Nika Club sailed down and complained and said they would publicize it in the papers if the girls weren't hired. So they were hired!" The Mika Nika Club, he explained, was formed recently following a panel discussion at the United church in the town. Indians had been invited to come, to answer questions from the audience. "The United church people were amazed at conditions; had thought things were all right with the Indians. At the end of the meeting, people who wanted to do something about it signed up to form this club. They got lots of signatures. The club meets regularly and will take up all matters in which Indians may need help. It has Indians and Whites and men and women in its membership."[3]

In addition to out-and-out job discrimination, Indians can encounter more subtle forms, paralleling those we have mentioned in the cases of school children. "Why," for instance, an Indian mother said indignantly, "do they have to print INDIAN on the chart at the foot of your bed in the hospital? They say it's needed for the medical payment, but that's not necessary! And when I took one of my children to the hospital, they asked me if I was legally married. This was insulting."

And Indians know that some of them can expect to be turned away from one of the two beer parlors, simply because they are Indians. "They're letting in only those they know and trust," an Indian explained.

If the White world is still not entirely accepting of the Indian, on the other hand it must be said that sometimes the Indians appear to move with reluctance—or perhaps timidity or lack of know-how—into areas of the White environment where they are invited. We have already suggested that they may have felt unable to handle the questionnaires sent to them regarding the after-school study group. And there are other instances of Indian failures to apply for privileges—the failure of a high school graduate to fill out the form that would guarantee for another year the job she loved as a teacher-aide; and failures of Indian parents to send in applications expressing choice of schools for their children. These may indeed be failures of know-how vis-à-vis the complications of paper work. Of a different nature was the refusal of mothers in the nursery

---

3. For a description of a very similar Mika Nika Club in the Kamloops area see H. B. Hawthorn, ed., *A Survey of the Contemporary Indians of Canada*, 2 vols. (Ottawa: Indian Affairs Branch, 1966), 1: 126.

school program to staff their exhibition booth in a town exhibition. No mother would agree either to man the booth or even to pour out a cup of tea that had already been prepared. Was this refusal due to "shyness," as the parent chairman thought? Perhaps the feelings involved were allied to those that keep the Indians sitting in the old Indian waiting room when they go to the clinic, instead of in the large general waiting room now open to all. The band council member who spoke to me about the Mika Nika Club commented very cogently on this clinic situation: "Even I—if there's a place in the Indian room—will sit there rather than go in with the White people. I don't know why. . . . I guess change has to come slowly. There are feelings of difference that are felt. An Indian feels different among Whites, just as he feels that a White on the reserve is different from the Indians." Actually there was a White man on the reserve at the time, living in common-law union in the home of an Indian woman. This situation was stirring up a good deal of criticism among the Indians.

It seems likely that as long as there are feelings of difference, the Indian ceremonies will continue to offer the Indian one of the strongest shields possible for his sense of pride. It must be remembered that the ceremonies link not only members of the Camas Band, but frequently involve the attendance of neighboring bands from the north and south and even from the mainland. In fact, in recent years participation of the neighboring bands has been much more widespread. In 1962 Suttles reported that twelve big dances were held that winter in nine different places, on nearly every Saturday night for a three-month period, with attendance that on several occasions must have been up to a thousand persons.[4] In 1968 Ryan reported to me that people from communities on the mainland who hadn't danced for years were attending the island dances and even beginning to build their own "smokehouses."[5]

---

4. Wayne Suttles, "The Persistence of Intervillage Ties Among the Coast Salish," *Ethnology* 2 (October 1963): 517.

5. Joan Ryan, personal communication.

EPILOGUE

Suttles' description of the big intertribal dances makes very explicit their nature as gatherings of a large group of people who feel themselves linked as kin. At a naming ceremony, for instance, classificatory terms of address (cousin, niece, nephew, uncle) are used by sponsors and witnesses throughout the speech-making. "The precise genealogical connection may not even be known. The point is that some relationship can be named, and thus through the sponsors of a big dance most or all of the groups of guests are linked. After several hours of this, one begins to see the whole area as one great kin group embracing several thousand people." [6]

We repeat, in 1968 the Camas Indian does indeed remain an Indian, bolstered by a large network of kin who make up his "community," bound through ties of blood, not of propinquity, and through ties of common purpose, resulting in affirmation of Indian identity and unity. Regarding this concept of "community," let me point out that the subdivision and the plan to "straighten up" the roads of Village I should not lead anyone to assume that the old pattern of Camas life is necessarily on its way out. True, parts of Village I may in time take on more of a superficial resemblance to the residential areas of the town. But there is no sign that the widespread kinship network, always of fundamental importance to the Camas, is losing its functions or its viability; no sign that the local neighborhood is assuming more significance than the "neighborhood" made up of the related groups residing up and down the coast. Indeed, in addition to the large gatherings for winter dancing, and in lesser degree for Shaker activities, Suttles points to the importance of still another mechanism for cementing traditional loyalties and bringing local groups together—the summer canoe race weekends, important at present in certain of the Salish vicinities.[7]

At the same time, while the Indian is strengthening his identity through traditionally Indian activities, we have seen that

6. Suttles, "Intervillage Ties," p. 520.
7. Ibid., p. 521.

he is acquiring new skills and experience in making joint efforts of many kinds, using the techniques of cooperating in councils, committees, associations, conferences. Some of these are local efforts—the band council and its committees, and the nursery school—with membership limited to Camas Indians; others, such as the Southern Vancouver Island Tribal Federation and the leadership conferences and workshops bring him into contact with Indians from other reserves, who may be either kin or non-kin. And the Mika Nika Club leads him into direct action with Whites.

The Indian's strengths, then, are growing. He has more avenues for group action toward improvement of his life. And there is evidence that he feels this strength and uses it, even in dramatic ways. The women "march" to make a demand; the Mika Nika Club assails a store owner to protest discrimination; a possibility is envisioned of band council resignations to protest the actions of the Minister of Indian Affairs; and an Indian stands up against a White anthropologist with a courteous but strong "No."

Suttles even observed a large dance gathering on Vancouver Island taking on the semblance of a political rally on one occasion in 1962. "White enemies" were named—meaning the "Indian agent" and his assistants, "who were said to be threatening to withhold social assistance from Indians participating in the winter dances. The gist of one speech was that a united effort might get the 'enemies' removed from their positions. So far as I know, nothing came of it. But on this occasion, for a few moments, the gathering was less a dance than a political rally."[8]

How will the Camas use their growing "Indian power" in the future? This remains an open question. So far, they have been fortunate among contemporary minority groups in that they have had access to strong kin ties within a strong ceremonial life, offering them prestige satisfactions and feelings of security in their own terms. They have been fortunate, too, that a steady —even though circumscribed—encouragement has been given

---

8. Ibid., p. 520.

to them to become more powerful as citizens; to make decisions and plans; and to develop their own leaders.

Yet still there are Indians for whom alcohol is a crippling problem; there are Indians whose inclinations and beliefs do not allow them to participate in the ceremonies. And still, underlying the entire picture, are the basic inequalities inherent in the reserve system itself. What happens in the future depends very much on what will be done to break down the remaining barriers and minimize the feelings of unequal status. And it depends crucially on what will be done for those who are now children, to influence the ways they are going to feel about themselves and their lives.

Not all of the children of 1954 have fared well. True, some of the girls have become teacher-aides and secretaries; this fall a daughter of one of the nursery school mothers is entering nurse's training; a young man assists the Indian Health Services nurse as a Community Health Worker; another is widely known as a very talented carver; other young men work regularly in the large mill eight miles away. But on the other hand, one of our youngsters, now a tall, inarticulate boy of nearly fifteen, has been dragging along through the grades; two are dead of leukemia; still another took his own life in an argument over his parentage; and a boy who tried schooling in Vancouver fell in with a fast, drug-using crowd and now languishes at home, ill and cursing the fate that made him an Indian.

Surely the schools have a critical role to play—as yet unrealized—in building confidence and pride in the Indian children from the very day of school entry. This role calls for greatly enlarged budgets for nursery schools, kindergartens, elementary schools, special services, and research related to learning. It calls for new uses of imagination in training teachers, in remaking curriculum, in envisioning new goals and methods, and especially in enlisting vital parent participation.

We have said it before, and we say it again as we come to the end of our "look at the Indians"—remembering vividly those independent, fearless children who first greeted us: For the Camas, pride is the hub; around it all revolves.

Index

Arensberg, Conrad M., 9n.1, 162n.21
Aristocrats, 18–19

Barnett, Homer G., 12n.3, 26–27, 36, 40, 110, 111, 112, 150, 151n.8, 153
Beer parlors, 3–4, 80, 84–85, 86, 101–2, 106, 158, 161, 168, 184, 216
Belshaw, C. S., 52n.6, 110, 159, 160, 161, 168, 186, 187
Benedict, Ruth, 24
Berrying, 9. *See also* Occupations
Big House, 7, 32–33, 62, 88; abandonment of, 47–48, 62; of Village I, 66, 199, 214
Black Hawks (gang), 100, 101, 168
Boas, Franz, 12n.1, 30, 34, 50
Boggs, Stephen T., 179
Brown, Robert, 51, 53

Camas Band, 8, 13, 29, 44–45, 56, 85–86, 166, 169, 219–20; band fund, 57, 136, 137, 184, 188; band list, 56–57; causes of death among, 59; chieftainship of, 57, 180, 183; Community Development Program, 200–201; cooperation among, 76–77, 143, 147, 180, 194, 195, 219; council of, 48, 49, 57, 70–71, 145, 183, 184, 188, 200–202; enfranchisement of, 56, 58, 114–15; intermarriage with non-Indians, 105, 107, 110, 111, 166; military service by, 59; mobility of, 186–87, 195; outside contacts of, 78–80, 83, 85, 183–84; political activity among, 144, 197, 219; reluctant to move into White environment, 216–17; residence system of, 114, 180; social organization, persistence of, 180–81, 218; subdivision, 200, 201, 202–5; in United States, 57, 67, 115; White contacts of, 81–82, 86, 109, 177–78, 185, 205, 212–13, 219
Camas Reserve, 46–47, 186–87; cemeteries on, 63, 64; new buildings on, 199; Village I, 61, 62–63, 64, 65-72, 73, 77, 82, 87, 120, 125–30 passim, 133, 136, 137, 164, 165, 193, 198, 199, 203, 214, 218; Village II, 117, 129–34, 137, 164, 183, 199; Village III, 63, 117; Village IV, 90; Village V, 199
Catholics, Indian, 7, 50, 54–55, 106, 109, 152
Change, cultural, 110, 111, 112, 119, 123–24, 182–83, 191, 193–94, 195–96
Children, 5, 31–32, 92–94, 102, 103–4, 119, 121, 220; birth and infancy, 33–34, 169–71; childhood, 35–37, 171–75; in disrupted homes, 139–40; in "fatherless" homes, 138–39; illegitimate, 129, 133–34; independence of, 178–79, 189; naming ceremony for, 34–35, 74, 107; puberty and adolescence, 37–39, 163–69, 177. *See also* Schools
Church, Catholic, 63, 77, 85, 135, 144, 161, 167. *See also* Shakers
Collins, June McCormick, 150, 152n.10

INDEX

Commoners, 19, 21
Comox, 14
Cooperation, economic, 20
Curtis, Edward S., 12n.2, 29

Dancer, new, 7, 24–27, 62, 74, 75, 76, 96, 149, 214
Dancing, 74–76, 82, 92, 94, 102, 107, 148, 156, 214–15
Dead: burial of, 43, 72–74, 88; fear of the, 31, 35, 88. *See also* Life after death; Murder
Debts, 20
Deity, 30
Devereux, George, 31n.23
Dialect, Camas, 59, 92
Discrimination, 80–81, 106, 212–14, 215, 216
Douglas, Sir James, 46
Drinking, 139–40, 144, 151, 152, 157–62, 197. *See also* Liquor
Du Bois, Cora, 179

Electricity in houses, 66, 103, 118, 183
Event analysis, 9

Family, 8, 35, 41–42, 141, 169; Gordon, 97, 98, 116, 118, 135, 138, 167, 198; Harry, 89, 94–95, 118, 141, 152, 166, 198; Farming, 47, 53, 54, 143 Wilson, 104–5, 147, 198–99
Father, 36, 174
Fishing rights, 54, 143
Food supply, 14, 15

Gambling, 22
Games, 36–37
Gangs, 100–101, 168
Ghosts, 31, 71, 103
Gift-giving, 17–18, 21, 30, 73–74, 75, 147, 180

Grandparents, 8, 35, 42–43, 44, 95, 119–21, 139
Gunther, Erna, 150

Hale, Horatio, 50
Halkomelem language, 59
Hawthorn, H. B., 52n.6, 110, 159, 160, 161, 168, 186, 187, 216n.3
Headman, 18–19, 21, 44, 47, 48; decline of authority of, 48, 49, 161
Health Regulations, Indian, 58
Homans, George C., 192n.5
Households, 18, 19, 47–48, 89, 97–98, 108–9, 114
Houses, 4–5, 16–17, 44, 47, 62, 66, 88–89, 97, 99, 104, 109, 113, 114, 115–18, 183, 185, 193, 198, 202–4

Independence and individualism, 156–57, 162–63, 170, 178–79, 220
Indian Act: of 1876, 47; of 1884, 49
Indian Agent. *See* Superintendent.
Indian Agency, 4, 9, 83–84
Informants, 9
Intermarriage, 20; with non-Indians, 105, 107, 110, 111, 166

Jamieson, S. M., 52n.6, 110, 159, 160, 161, 168, 186, 187

Kimball, Solon T., 9n.2, 162n.21
Kinship system, 15–18, 43–44, 65, 86, 180, 193, 218; impact of Whites on, 48–49; in Village I, 67–70, 71, 72, 73
Kwakiutl, 14, 24

222

INDEX

Land: allotments, 64–65;
disputes over, 51–53, 54;
ownership of, 47, 49, 97,
141–42, 185, 186, 187; taken
by White settlers, 46–47,
52–53, 60
Lane, Barbara, 12n.4, 26, 27, 30,
74, 149
Language, Indian, 59, 62
Lemert, Edwin M., 153, 157,
158–59, 160n.18
Lewis, Claudia, 208n.1
Life after death, 31
Liquor, sale of to Indians:
permitted, 197; prohibited, 46,
54, 58, 86, 159, 188–89
Location tickets, 47, 49, 67

MacGregor, Gordon, 169n.25
MacIver, R. M., 118
Magic, 27–29
Malinowski, Bronislaw, 181, 183
Marriage, 7–8, 35, 37–40, 44, 163;
arranged, 121–22, 167; by
Indian ceremony, 137–38, 214;
with non-Indians, 105, 107,
110, 111, 166; outside of band,
78, 135, 136, 137, 165; patterns
of, 95–96, 97, 99, 105, 125–38,
164–66; preparation of girls
for, 37–38, 120, 164;
termination of, 40, 122
Mead, Margaret, 194n.7
Medium, 28
Men: employment of, 142–43;
land-owning by, 141–42;
status of, 41, 144–46
Menomini Indians, 181–82
Menstruation, first, 37
Mika Nika Club, 215–16, 219
Missionaries, Catholic, 46, 50,
54

Morrison, Frank, 12n.5, 31n.21,
55n.12
Mother, 35, 36
Murder, 20, 29

Names, 59; great, 20–21
Naming ceremony, 7, 214, 218;
of child, 34–35, 74, 107;
of adolescent boy, 39
Native Brotherhood of British
Columbia, 144, 195
Newspapers, items relating to
Indians in, 183–84, 185
Nootka, 14
North American Indian
Brotherhood, 144, 195

Occupations, 53, 66–67, 78, 79,
80–81, 90–91, 97, 105–6,
106–7, 142–43, 187, 197, 215,
220

Peall, Hubert, 59–60
Pearson, Marion, 9n.2
Potlatch, 18, 20, 21, 22, 34–35,
46, 54; forbidden, 49–50, 180
Protestant United Church
Mission, 64
Puyallup, 21, 22

Rattles, 146
Rees, Alwyn D., 194n.6
Relief. *See* Welfare
Reincarnation, 31
Research methodology, 9–11
Ritualists, 28
Ryan, Joan, 217

Salish Indians, 3, 13, 24, 29, 36,
218; of Puyallup, 28; of
Lummi, 29, 53–54
Sapir, Edward, 195

223

INDEX

Schools, 78, 90, 95, 99–100, 102, 105, 108–9, 163–64, 167, 175–77, 189–91, 205, 220; adult education, 210–12; after-school study program, 210; Catholic, 50–51, 59, 63, 78, 79, 176, 199; compulsory, 58–59, 163; discrimination in, 212–14; nursery, 207–10; orientation class, 207; Protestant, 51, 59, 78; public, 81–82, 199, 206, 207; receiving home, 210
Seer, 28
Shaman, 27
Shakers, Indian, 55, 64, 71–72, 85, 94, 123, 135, 144, 150–57, 168, 195, 199
Slaves, 19
Smith, Marian, 21, 22n.8, 28
Songs, 7, 25–26, 73, 92, 153, 156, 163
Southern Vancouver Island Tribal Federation, 202, 219
Spindler, George D., 181n.2
Spirit dance, 26
Spirit helper, 22–24, 26, 38–39
Spirit power, 23, 44, 102, 148–49
Sports, 79, 109, 168
Status, 20, 44, 107, 108, 111–12, 147, 157, 158–59, 185, 220; linked to age, 145; relative to Whites, 86, 107–8, 114, 115, 204; rise in, 23–24
Superintendent (Indian Agent), 47, 48–50, 52, 54, 57, 183–84, 196, 219
Suttles, Wayne, 19n.7, 29, 53, 55, 217, 218, 219

Swaihwe masks, 39, 74, 146
Sweater trade, 124. *See also* Women, work of

Taboos, 43
Tamanawas dance, 49, 50
Town, 192–93, 199
Tuberculosis, 139

Underhill, Ruth, 34

Vancouver Island, 3, 14
Villages, 14–18 passim. *See also under* Camas Reserve
Voget, Fred W., 150, 151, 157

Wages, 53
Warfare, 29
Water in houses, 66, 116, 117, 183, 203
Water travel, 14
Wealth, 20. *See also* Potlatch
Welfare, 4, 57–58, 91, 143, 188, 197
Whites, 46–60 passim; early settlers, 46–47, 52–53, 60; impact on kinship system, 48–49; obligations to Indians, 191. *See also* Camas band, White contacts of
Winter ceremonies, 7, 24, 27, 62, 74–76, 86, 96, 107, 109, 145, 146–50, 167–68, 180, 214, 217–18; children excluded from, 35
Women: appearance of, 122; status of, 41, 123, 141, 144, 145, 193; work of, 40–41, 50, 106, 119, 124–25, 193